MATCHING
CAST ONS & BIND OFFS

MATCHING
CAST ONS & BIND OFFS

Six More Pairs of Methods
that Form Identical Cast On and Bind Off Edges
on Projects Knitted Flat and in the Round

Maryna Shevchenko

10 Rows a Day

www.10rowsaday.com

ISBN 978-1-7386402-4-9 paperback
ISBN 978-1-7386402-5-6 e-book

Cover design by:
Sasha Shevchenko
www.sasha-shevchenko.com

Published in Canada

To everyone
who finds joy in knitting

CONTENTS

INTRODUCTION

In the first part of the "Matching Cast Ons and Bind Offs" book, we discussed three pairs of cast-on and bind-off methods that form identical basic edges and three pairs of methods that make the edges look like i-cords.

This time around, we'll explore six more pairs of methods that create a matching look at the horizontal edges of our projects.

In the first section of this book, we'll talk about ways to turn cast-on and bind-off edges into decorative elements. These are the edges that transform even the most basic of projects into exquisite creations.

First, we'll see how we can make elegant double-chain edges. Then we'll discuss the picot edge that designers often add to their most well-crafted knits. Finally, we'll take the idea of decorative edgings one step further when we discuss edges formed by criss-cross cast-on and bind-off methods.

In the second section of this book, we'll talk about edges that do not look like edges at all. They do not end at the top or at the bottom of a project. Rather, they seem to be flowing around the fabric continuously.

We'll see how we can apply these methods to projects worked back and forth and to the ones worked in the round.

When you are choosing the perfect cast-on and bind-off pair for your project, you'll be able to easily assess each method by looking at the close-up photo and the icons depicting the stretch, the level of difficulty, and the tools used to work each method. All of this at-a-glance information is provided on the title page of each matching cast-on and bind-off duo.

To help you remember each method described in this book, I created quick reference cards with step-by-step photos and short instructions that explain how each method works. Feel free to cut those cards out of the book to keep them on hand when you use these methods to enhance your knitted creations.

Happy knitting, my friend!

Maryna

DECORATIVE EDGES

DOUBLE-CHAIN CAST ON
AND DOUBLE-CHAIN BIND OFF

STRETCH ★★★★☆

DIFFICULTY ★★☆☆☆

TOOLS

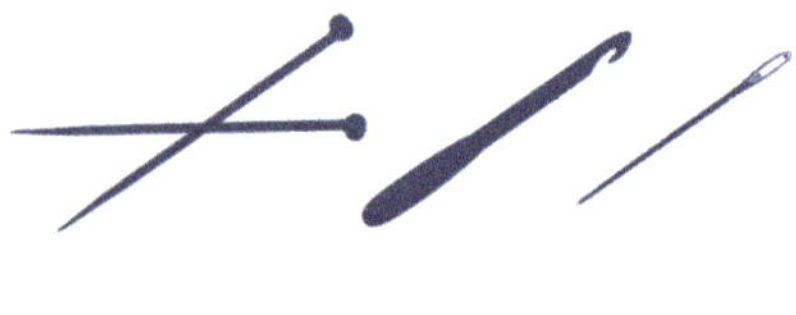

We'll start by discussing a pair of methods that make the horizontal edges of our projects **look like two chains** of stitches placed next to each other, with one chain running from left to right and the other one from right to left.

These **edges are identical** on the right and wrong sides of the work, and that makes them perfect for blankets, scarves and other projects that proudly show off both sides of the fabric.

DOUBLE-CHAIN CAST ON WORKED FLAT

They say that this method was **demonstrated by a Chinese waitress** to a knitter who was dining at a Beijing restaurant where that waitress worked.

Whether it is true or not, the name stuck, and now we often refer to this technique as the **Chinese Waitress Cast On**, even though a more technical name for this method is Double-Chain Cast On.

Since it was first described in the "Cast On, Bind Off" book by Cap Sease, this way to cast on stitches was **improved and simplified**.

We don't need to untwist the chain after we cast on each stitch, we don't need to make a slip knot and unravel it after we work the first row, and we **use a crochet hook** and a knitting needle to make the process of casting on stitches much easier.

The size of the chains formed at the bottom of the edge is **determined by the size of the crochet hook** that we use.

To make an edge that is approximately as loose as the main fabric of the future project, use a **hook that is two sizes smaller** than the size of the needles you plan to use. For example, to cast on stitches for the swatch shown in the photos, I used a **10mm (US size 15)** knitting needle and an **8mm (US size L11)** crochet hook.

If you are after a **looser, more elastic edge**, use a hook in the same size as the needles. For a **tighter edge**, use a much smaller hook.

Place a crochet hook **at the right-hand side** of the knitting needle so that the head of the hook is facing up and its **"nose" is facing you**. Hold the hook and the needle in your **left hand.**

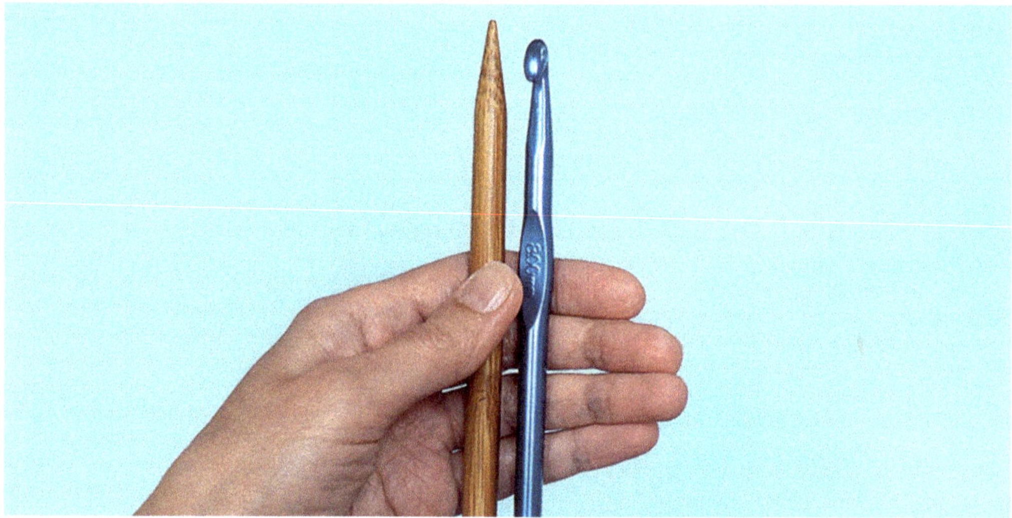

Place the working yarn in your left palm so that the yarn tail runs down your palm and the **strand is at the back** of the hook and the needle.

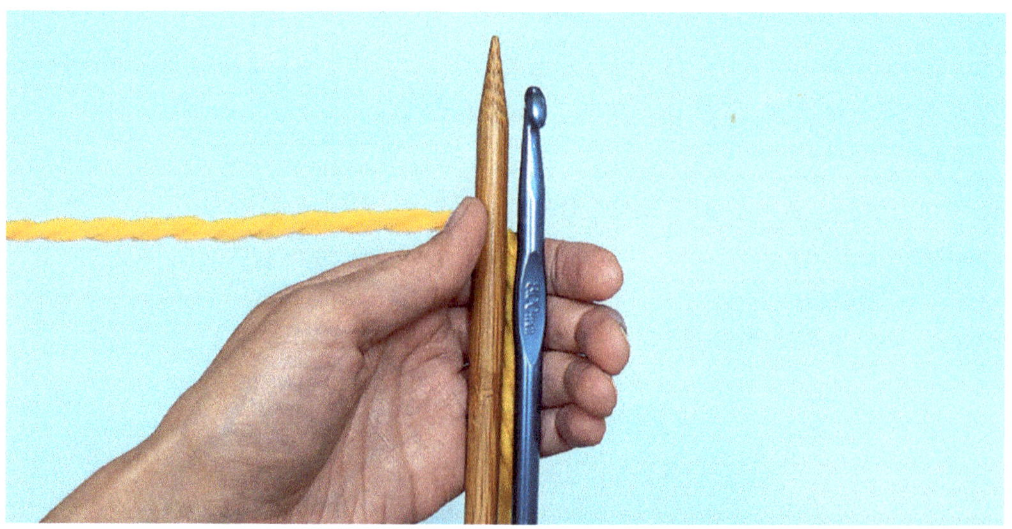

Hold the tools and the yarn tightly **in your left hand**.

This cast-on method **does not require a long tail**, so there is no need to worry that we will run out of yarn before we cast on all the stitches that we need for our project.

STEP 1

Take the working yarn in your right hand and **wrap it around both tools** from the back, **to the right,** to the front, to the left, and finally to the back.

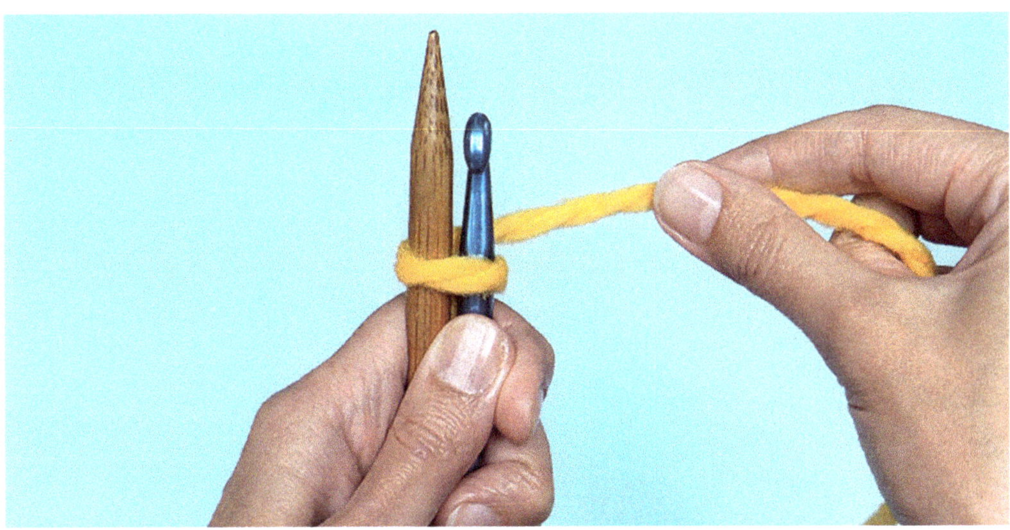

Repeat this sequence again to **make the second wrap**.

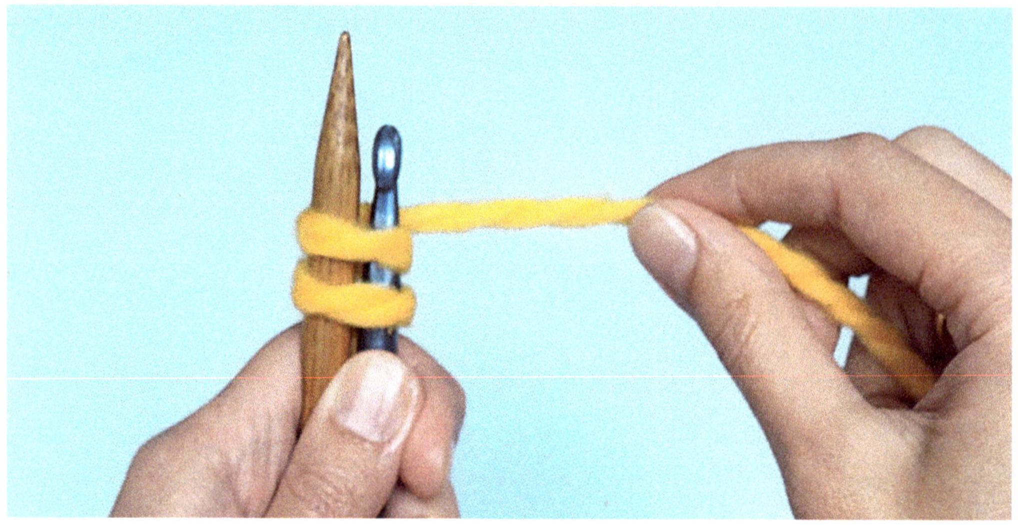

Make sure the **wraps do not overlap**. The second wrap should stay above the first one.

STEP 2

Take the crochet **hook in your right hand** and pull it down until the nose of the hook catches the second yarn wrap.

Twist the hook a bit to the left and move it down, **pulling the second yarn wrap through** the first one.

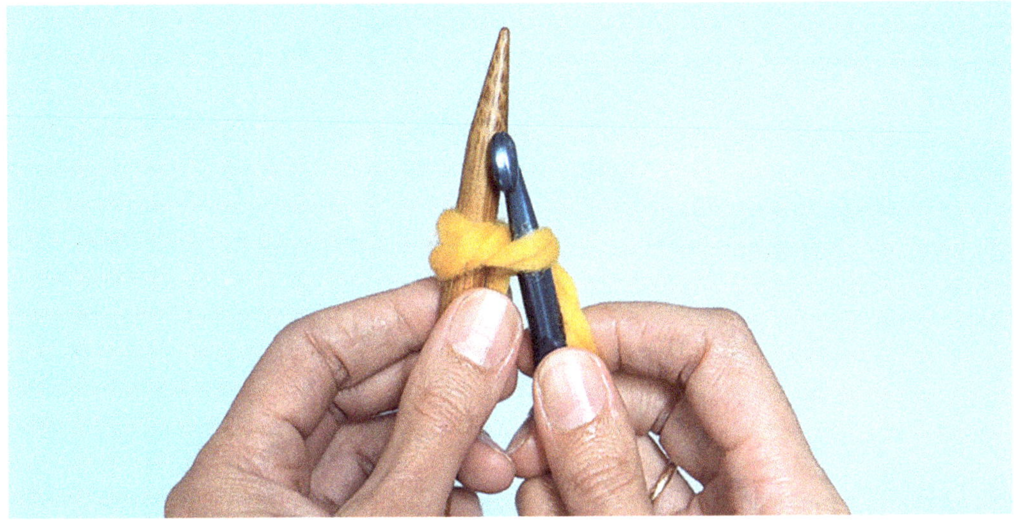

STEP 3

Return the crochet **hook back to your left hand** and move the working yarn to the front, **undoing what is left of the second wrap**.

Then move the **yarn to the back through the slot** between the needle and the head of the hook.

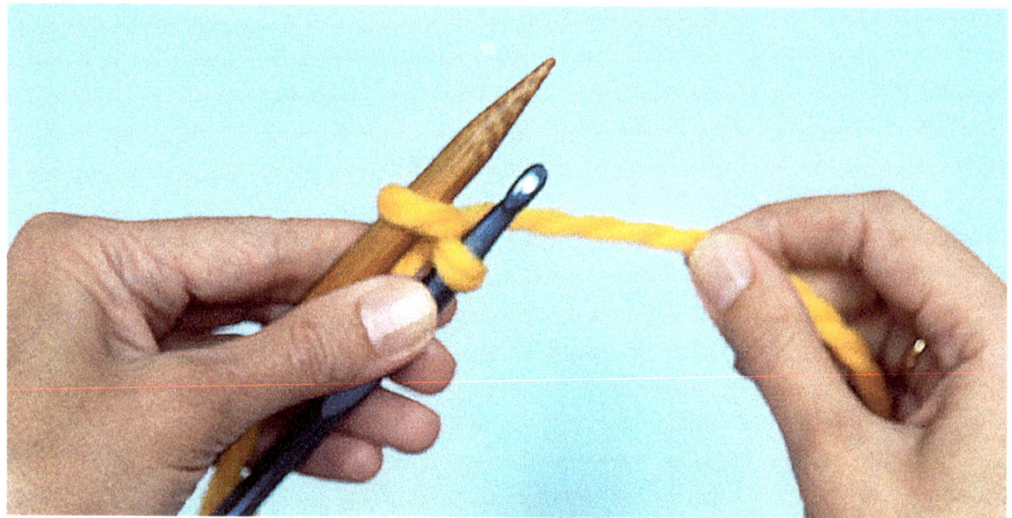

Now we are **back to the initial setup**—the needle and the hook are aligned in our left hand, and the **yarn is at the back** of the work. But this time, we have one stitch on the knitting needle and one stitch on the crochet hook.

Repeat steps 1 through 3 to **add one more stitch** to the knitting needle.

When you work **step 2 again**, pull the second yarn wrap **through both the first yarn wrap and through the stitch** sitting on the crochet hook.

Work steps 1, 2, and 3 repeatedly until your knitting needle holds **the number of stitches** that you need for your project **minus one stitch**. That last stitch is the one sitting on the crochet hook. To finish off the cast on, we need to transfer this stitch to the knitting needle.

To do this, take the crochet **hook in your right hand** (make sure you performed step 3 and the yarn has been moved through the space between the needle and the hook **to the back** of the work).

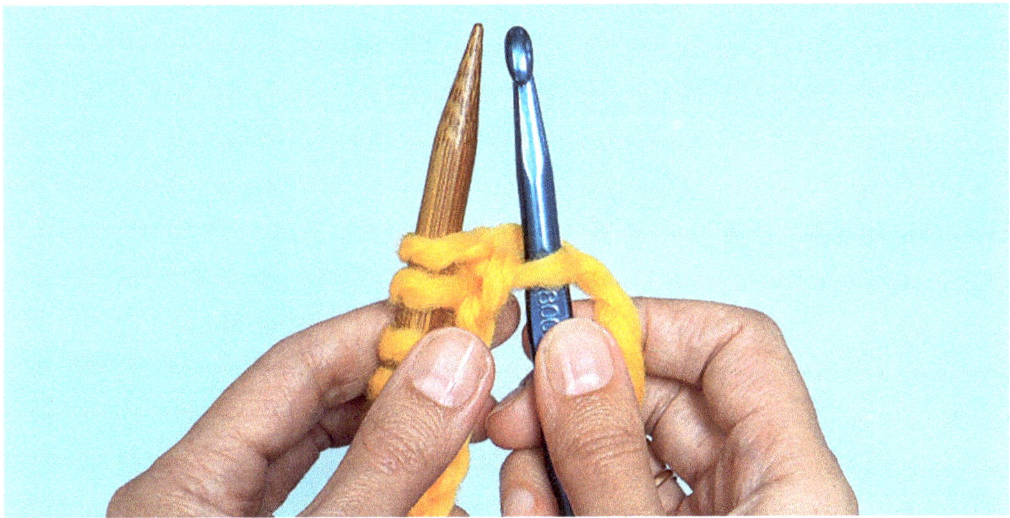

Then insert the tip of the knitting needle **from right to left** into the stitch on the crochet hook.

Ease the crochet hook out of that stitch and pull the yarn to **adjust the size of the last stitch**.

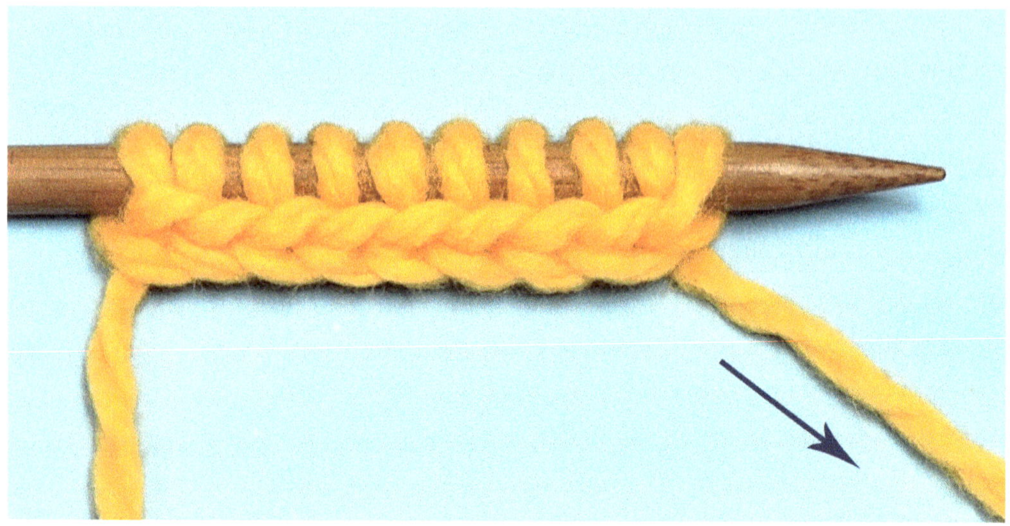

Now you have **all the stitches** that you need sitting **on the left needle**, and you can start to **work the first row** of your project right away.

DOUBLE-CHAIN CAST ON WORKED IN THE ROUND

To cast on stitches for a seamless project, **leave a longer yarn tail** hanging down your left palm before you cast on the first stitch, and then **use the same steps** as the ones we followed when we used double-chain cast on to get the initial set of stitches **for a project worked flat**.

Once you cast on the number of stitches that you need minus one stitch, **transfer the last stitch** from the crochet hook to the left needle.

Arrange all stitches on the needles using **any setup that allows us to work in the round**—double-pointed needles, two circular needles, one short circular needle, or split stitches in half on one long circular needle used with the magic loop method.

Don't join stitches in any special way. Simply make sure the cast-on **edge is not twisted** around the needles, and start to **work the first round** of your project.

To eliminate the gap between the first and last cast-on stitches, slightly **pull the working yarn** after you work the first stitch.

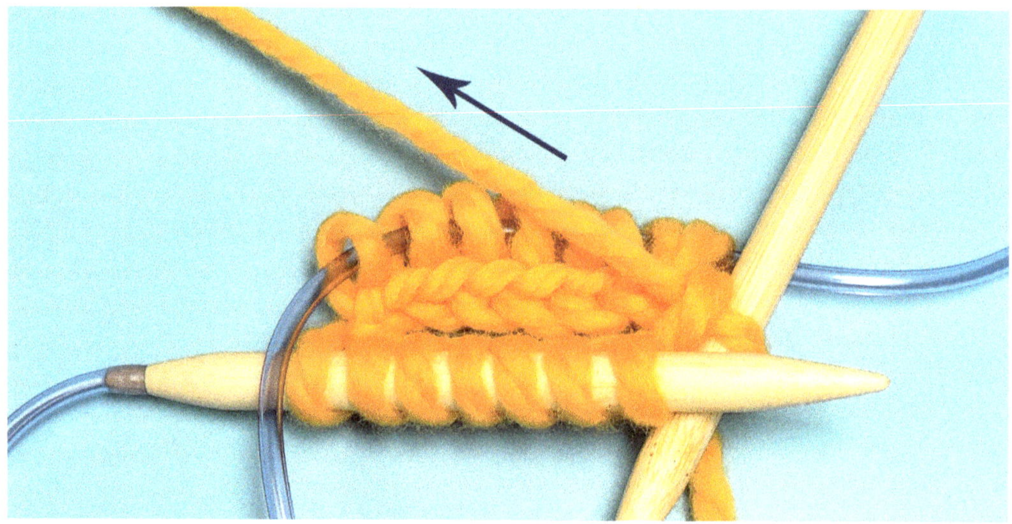

Continue to **work in the main pattern** of your project for a few rounds. Once there is some fabric formed at the top of the cast-on edge, we can **join the edge** in a way that is completely invisible.

You can also do this **after the project is finished**, but I often can't wait that long to see how the cast-on edge locks in a fully seamless circle.

Here's how we make it happen.

SETUP

Thread the yarn tail into a wool needle, and place the project so that the **cast-on edge is at the top** of the main fabric and the right side of the project is facing you.

To make it easier for you to see how to seamlessly join this cast on edge, I will use **yarn in a contrasting colour** as the yarn tail.

Make sure the yarn tail is **between the two legs of the first stitch** of the chain at the right-hand side of the gap.

STEP 1

Insert the wool needle **from front to back** under both legs of the **first full stitch** of the chain at the left-hand side of the yarn tail. Make sure you use the first full stitch, **not the half-stitch** that is stretched between the first and last stitches that we cast on.

Pull the yarn through, but **don't pull it too tight**. The strand that you form should be as big as **one leg of an average stitch** that forms the cast on edge.

STEP 2

Insert the wool needle **from front to back** into the spot where the yarn tail originated. This spot is **in the middle of the first full stitch** at the right-hand side of the edge.

Pick up the **inner leg of that stitch** and the strand that is right below it on the wrong side of the fabric.

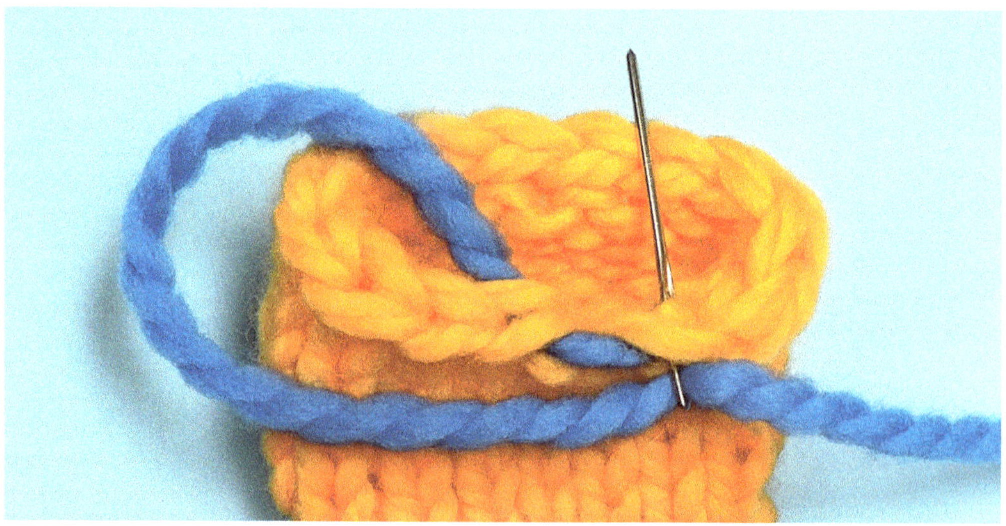

Pull the yarn through, making sure the strand that you form is **as long as one leg of any stitch** of the chain.

STEP 3

Finally, insert the wool needle **from front to back** into the spot where that yarn tail exited after we performed step 1, and pick the **strand that is right below** that spot.

Pull the yarn through and **adjust the length of the strand** to make it blend in with the rest of the chain.

Hide the yarn tail **within the cast-on edge**.

When we make this seam with the yarn in the same colour as the project, the edge looks like an **uninterrupted seamless circle**.

No matter what project you **choose to decorate** with this interesting (and easy!) cast-on method, you can be confident that the **edge looks neat on both sides** of the fabric and has **enough stretch** to support the main fabric of your knitting creation in the best possible way.

DOUBLE-CHAIN BIND OFF WORKED FLAT

There are several ways to add a double chain to a bind-off edge. The method that **creates an identical edge** to the one formed by the double-chain cast on involves an **unusual way to purl** stitches.

This approach to purling is used in Eastern knitting, and **it is a trick** that makes the double-chain bind off a **perfect match** to the double-chain cast-on method that we discussed in the first part of this chapter.

Here's how we can form this edge **step by step**.

STEP 1

With the right side of the fabric facing you, bring the **yarn to the front** of the work and insert the tip of the right needle **from right to left** into the first stitch on the left needle.

Then place the working yarn **underneath** the tip of the right needle.

This is the **Eastern purling** that I mentioned earlier. The difference between the Eastern and the classic purl is in **the way we wrap** the tip of the right needle with the yarn.

In classic knitting, we make the wrap **from the top of the right needle**, while in Eastern knitting we keep the yarn **at the bottom** of the tip of the right needle.

This subtle change creates stitches that **look neate**r. Plus, this way of purling is **a bit easier** than the method used in the classic knitting style.

Push the tip of the **right needle to the back** to turn the yarn wrap into a purl stitch. Then slip the just-purled stitch off the left needle.

STEP 2

Make a **regular yarn over** by bringing the yarn from the front over the top of the right needle, to the back of the needle, and **to the front** of the work.

STEP 3

Purl the next stitch using the **Eastern method** described in step 1

Now we have **two stitches and a yarn over** on the right needle, and it is time to bring them down to one stitch. We'll do it in the next two steps.

STEP 4

Insert the tip of the left needle from left to right **into the yarn over** that we formed in step 2.

Pass it over the first stitch from the tip of the right needle and off the needle.

We are left with **two stitches on the right needle**, but our target is to have one stitch, so let's bind off one more stitch.

STEP 5

Insert the tip of the left needle from left to right **into the second stitch** from the tip of the right needle.

Pass this stitch over the other stitch and off the needle.

Voila—there is **only one stitch** sitting on the right needle.

Repeat **steps 2 through 5,** making a yarn over, purling one stitch the Eastern way, and finally, binding off the yarn over and one stitch, bringing the number of stitches on the right needle to one.

When you bind off all stitches and there is only **one stitch left** on the right needle, **cut the yarn**, pass the yarn tail through the last stitch, and pull tight to secure.

DOUBLE-CHAIN BIND OFF WORKED IN THE ROUND

To form this edge when we bind off stitches of a **seamless project**, follow the steps required for adding double-chain bind off to a project worked flat (see **steps 1 through 5** described on pages 25-28).

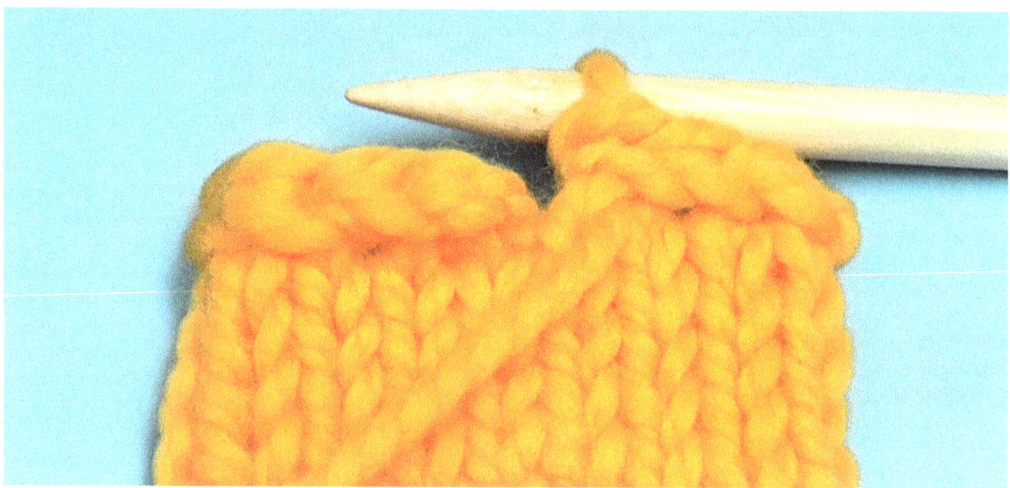

When you are left with one stitch sitting on the right needle, cut the yarn, leaving a **yarn tail around 20 cm / 8" long**. Pass the yarn tail through the last stitch and pull it just enough to make the last stitch **as big as the rest of the stitches** that form the chain.

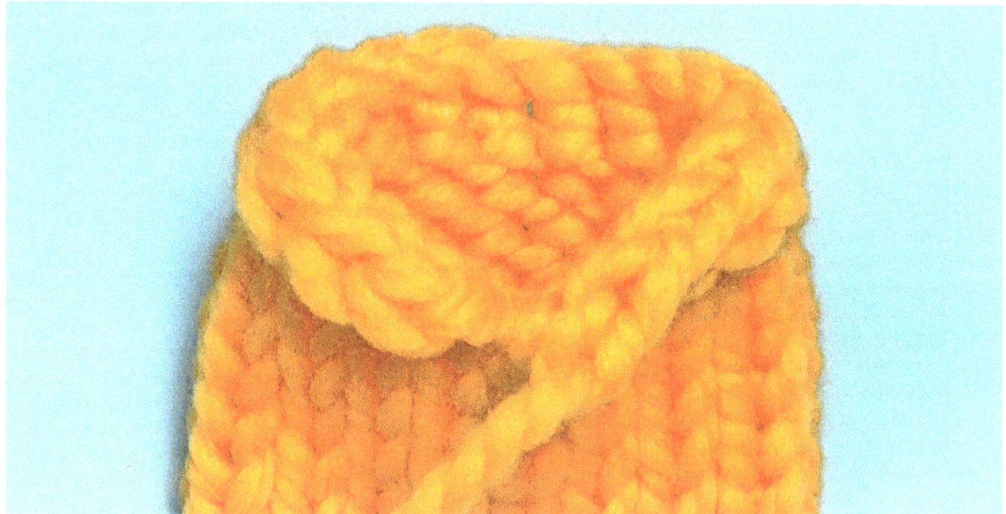

We'll join the double chains at the bind-off edge **the same way** as we stitched the chains at the cast-on edge into a seamless circle, but this time, we'll do it with the **wrong side of the fabric facing** us.

SETUP

Thread the yarn tail into a wool needle and place the project so that the **bind-off edge is at the top** and the wrong side of the fabric is facing you.

To make it easier for you to see each step of seaming, I'll use a piece of **yarn in a contrasting colour** as my yarn tail.

STEP 1

Insert the wool needle **from the bottom up** under the two legs of the first full stitch of the chain at the right-hand side of the yarn tail.

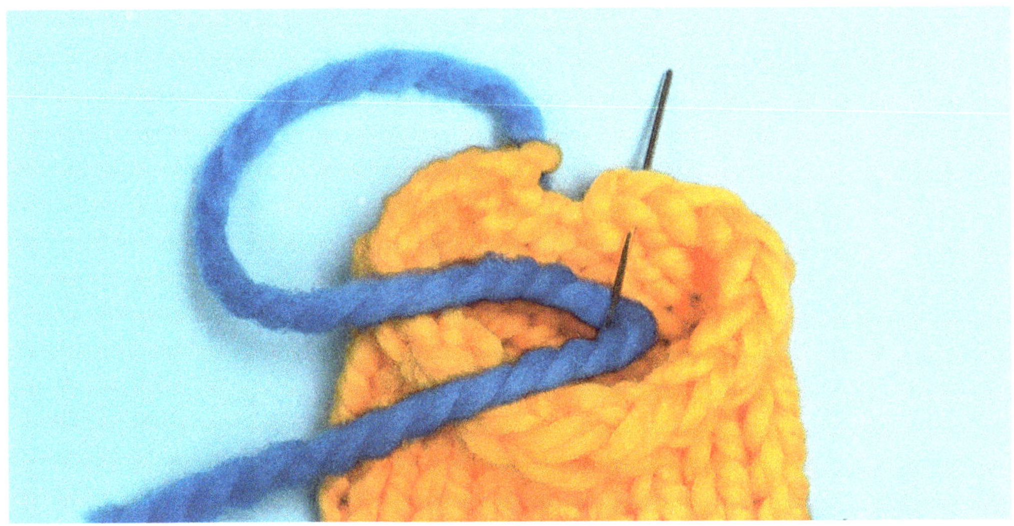

Pull the yarn through, forming a strand that is **as long as one leg of an average stitch** of the chain.

STEP 2

Insert the wool needle **from front to back** under the back leg of the last full stitch (the spot where the yarn tail originated) and under the strand that is **right below that leg** on the right side of the work.

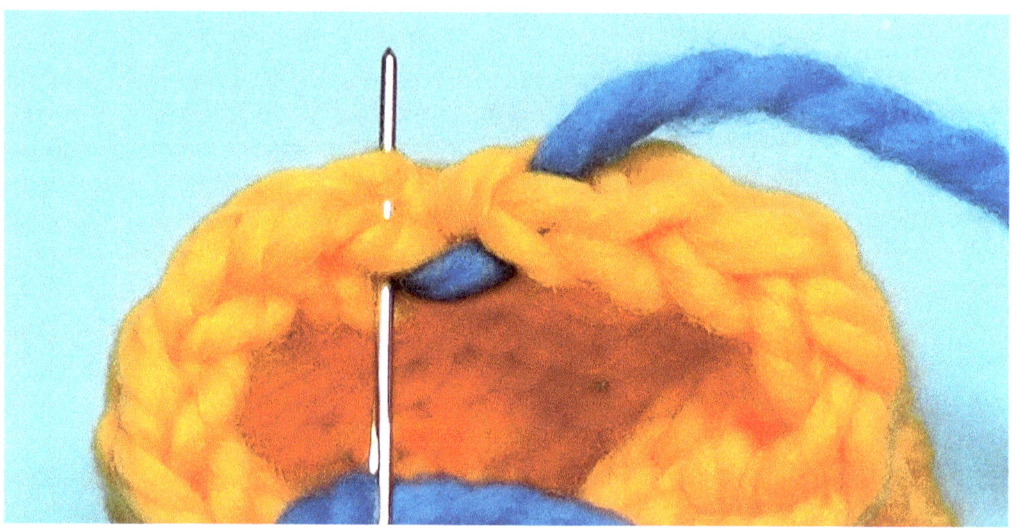

These two strands form the **last full stitch of the chain** that runs on the right side of the fabric.

Pull the yarn through, making sure the **new strand blends in** with the stitches of the chain.

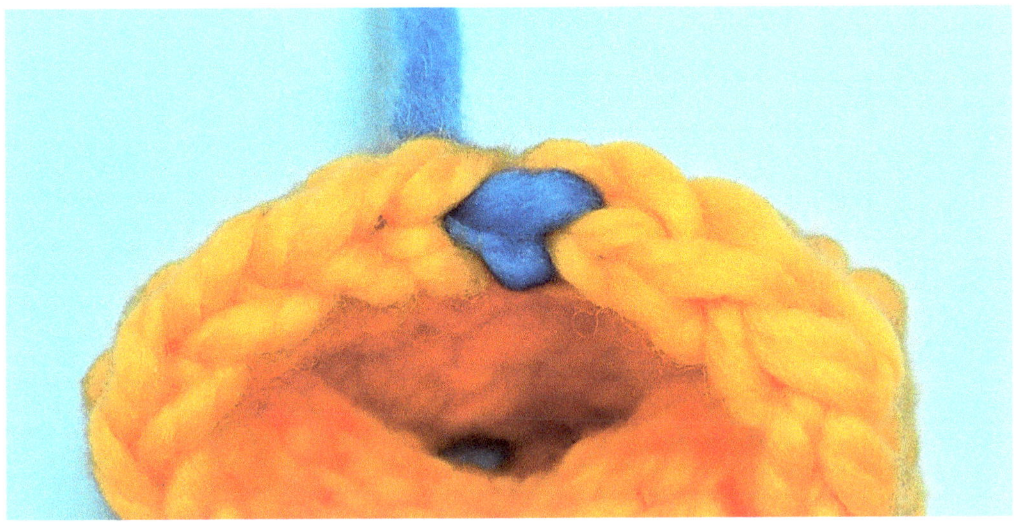

STEP 3

Go to the **first full stitch of the same chain** (it will be at the right-hand side of the yarn tail) and insert the wool needle **under the back leg** of that stitch.

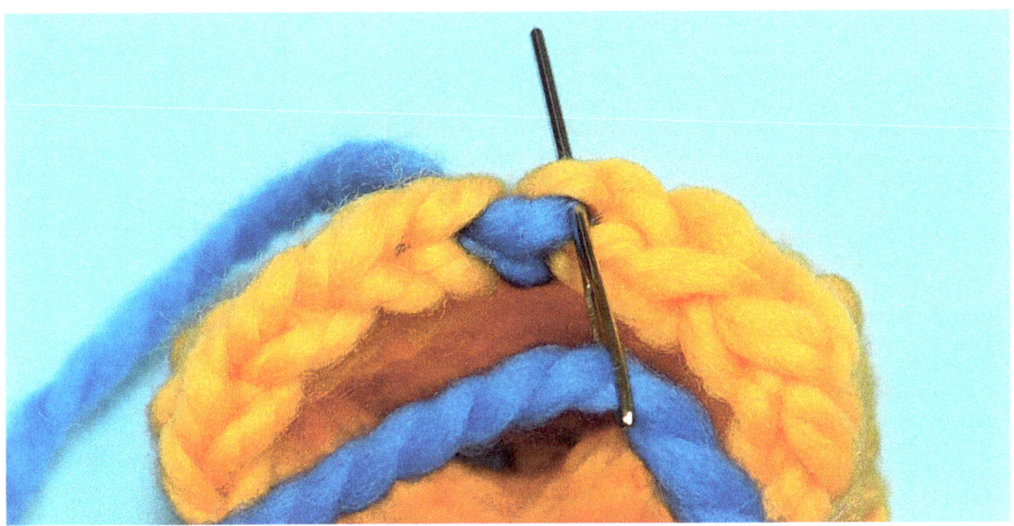

Pull the yarn through and **adjust the size of the strand** to make it as long as one leg of an avarage stitch of the chain.

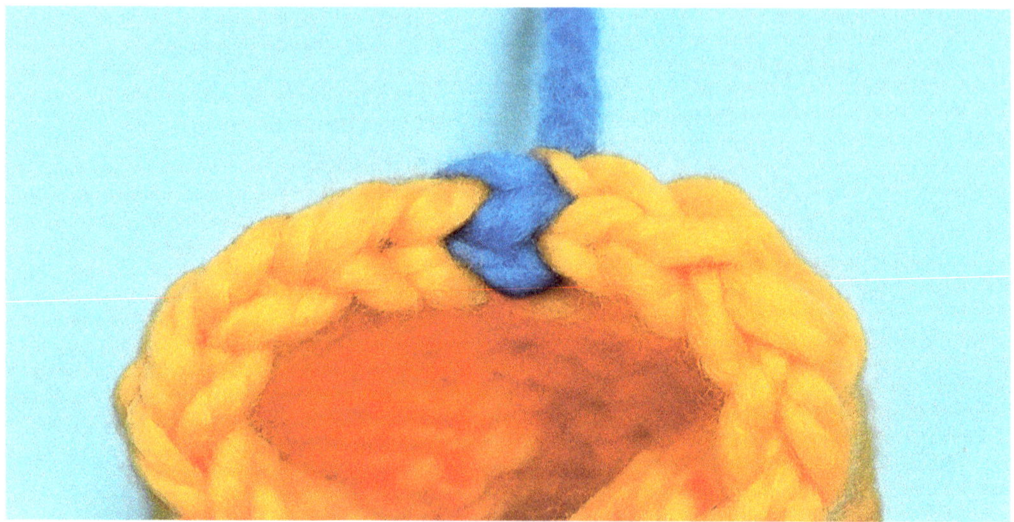

Secure the yarn and **hide the tail** on the wrong side of the fabric, or inside the bind-off edge.

Because I used yarn in a contrasting colour, you can clearly see where the seam is, but when the edge is joined with the **yarn in the same colour as the project,** it is absolutely invisible.

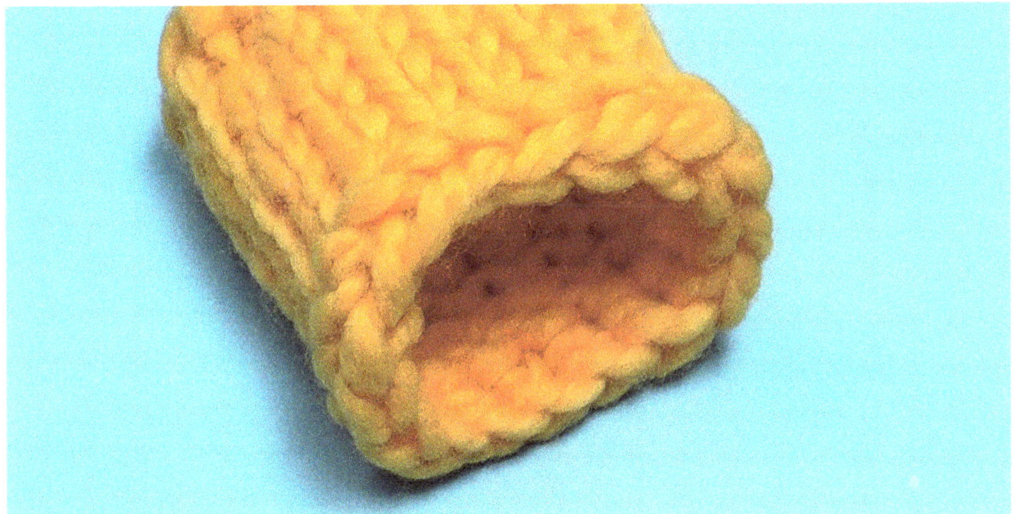

When you inspect the cast-on and bind-off edges, you will see that they are **mirror versions of each other**.

Everything is the same—two chains placed next to each other, the size of stitches in each chain, even the direction of the chains at the cast-on and bind-off edges is identical—**a perfect match**.

PICOT CAST ON
AND PICOT BIND OFF

STRETCH ★★★☆☆

DIFFICULTY ★★★☆☆

TOOLS

If you want to decorate your project with horizontal edges that look like **two strings of beads**—one at the bottom, and one at the top of the fabric—the Picot Cast On and Bind Off duo will be **perfect for the job**.

The edges formed by these methods look great on hats, cottage socks, mittens, sweaters, cardigans and pretty much anything else. The edges are **textured and quite elastic,** and they don't stretch out.

PICOT CAST ON WORKED FLAT

Out of all methods that allow us to make picot cast-on edge, the way described in this chapter takes the **least amount of time**.

The edging is formed **in two rows** that add texture to the fabric without making it too bulky. We do it by **pulling yarn** from around the cast on edge. This little trick is necessary for forming a lovely picot edge, which is the pride and joy of this cast-on method

STEP 1. CAST ON

Use the **slingshot version of the long-tail cast-on** method described below to cast on the number of stitches that you need for your project.

Start by measuring a long yarn tail. It should be about **four times as long** as the length of the cast-on edge.

Then place the working **yarn on your left index finger** and the yarn **tail on your left thumb**. Hold the tail and the working yarn with the other left fingers.

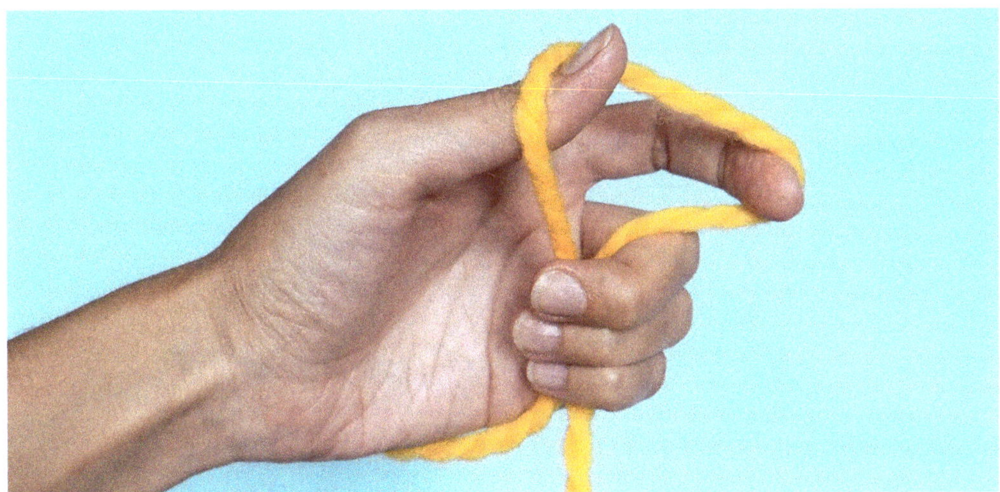

Take a knitting needle in your right hand and **place it on top** of the strand stretched between your left thumb and your index finger. Push the needle down to **make the strand form a V shape**.

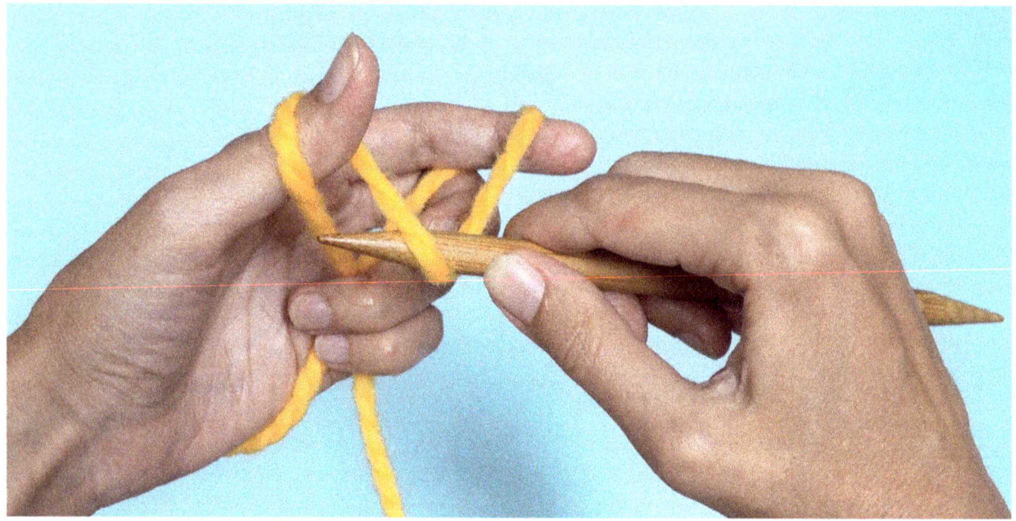

Now we are ready to cast on stitches.

1.1. First, insert the tip of the needle **from the bottom up** into the loop formed around your left thumb.

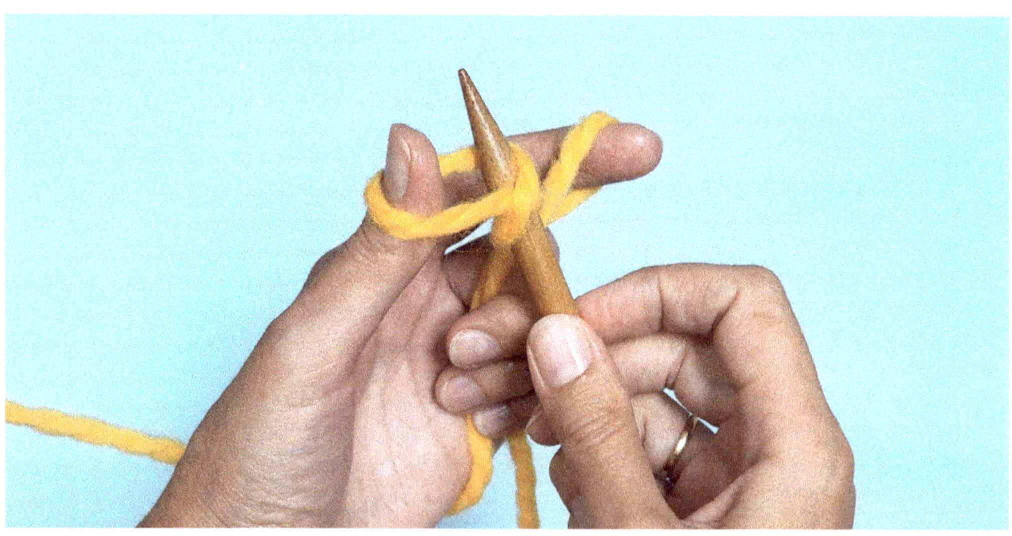

1.2. Pick the working yarn **from right to left**.

1.3. Pull the yarn through the loop.

1.4. Take your thumb **out of the loop** and put it into the space between the working yarn and the yarn tail.

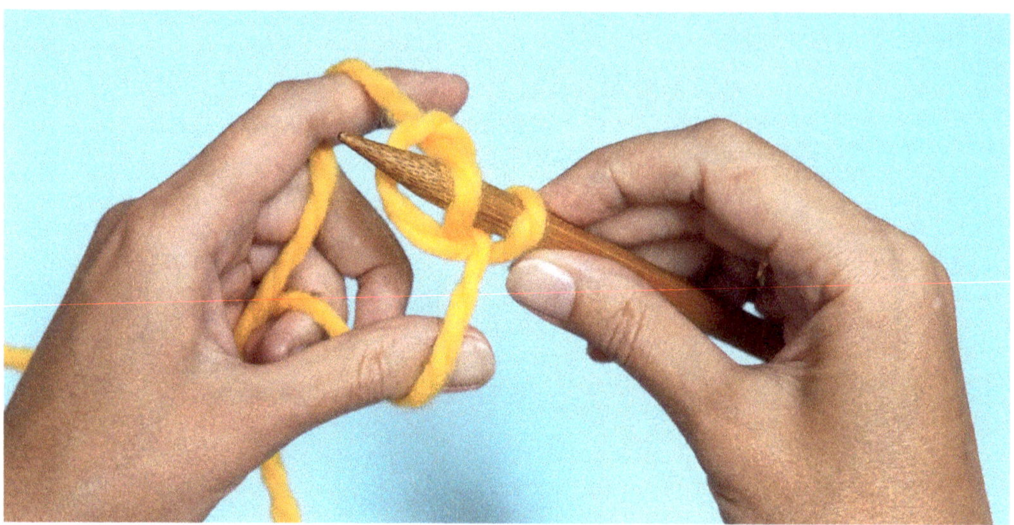

1.5. Finally, stretch your thumb and your index finger to **pull the strands apart** and close the loop at the bottom of the new stitch.

Repeat **steps 1.1 through 1.5** to cast on more stitches. At first, you will form two stitches at once, and then you will be adding **one more stitch** every time you repeat these steps.

I plan to make my swatch **10 stitches wide**, so that is the number of stitches I cast on.

STEP 2. ROW 1. WRONG SIDE OF THE WORK

In this step, we'll **pull the yarn from around the cast-on edge,** forming lovely picots and adding stitches to the work.

2.1. Knit 1 stitch.

2.2. Move the tip of the right needle down and to the back of the cast on edge.

2.3. Wrap the working yarn around the tip of the right needle the same way as we do when we knit a stitch.

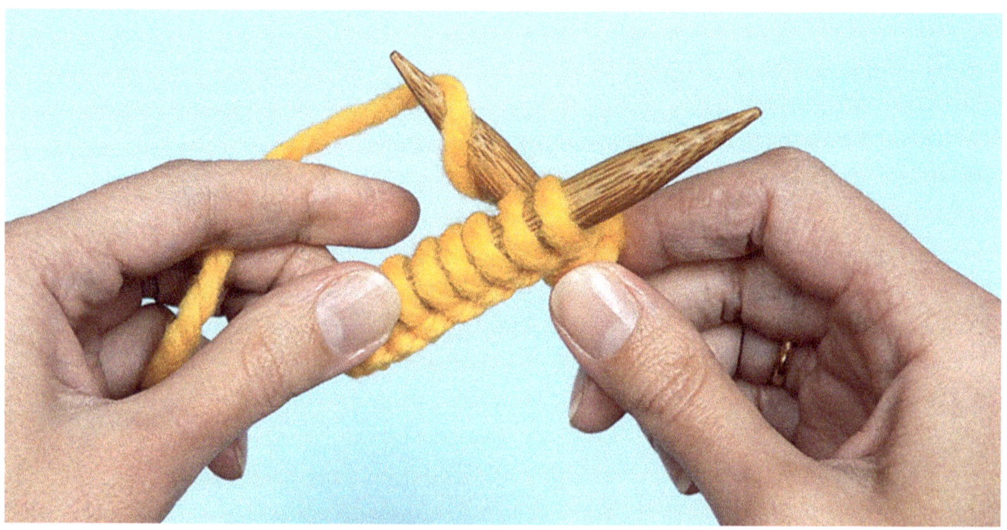

2.4. Move the tip of the right needle (with the wrap on it) from under the cast on edge **to the front of the work**.

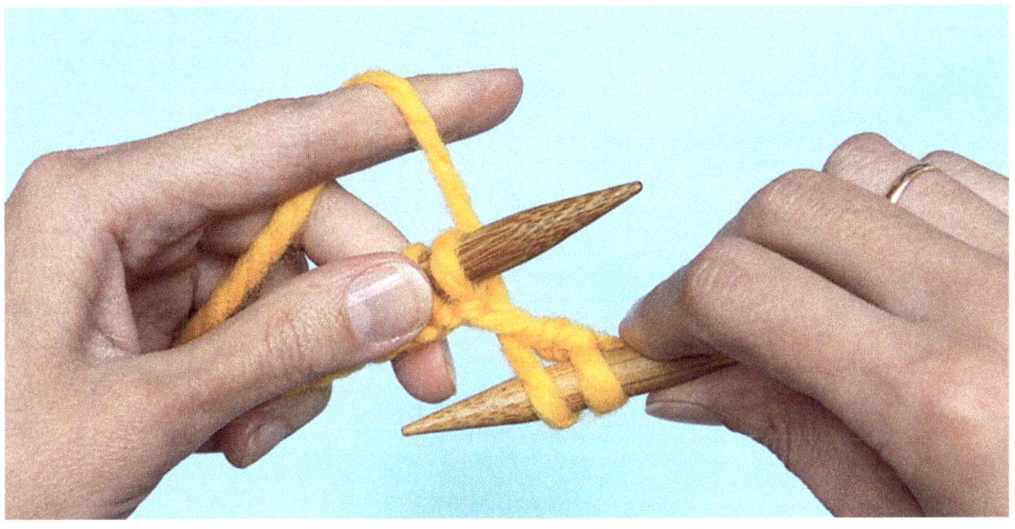

Repeat **steps 2.1 through 2.4** to the last stitch.

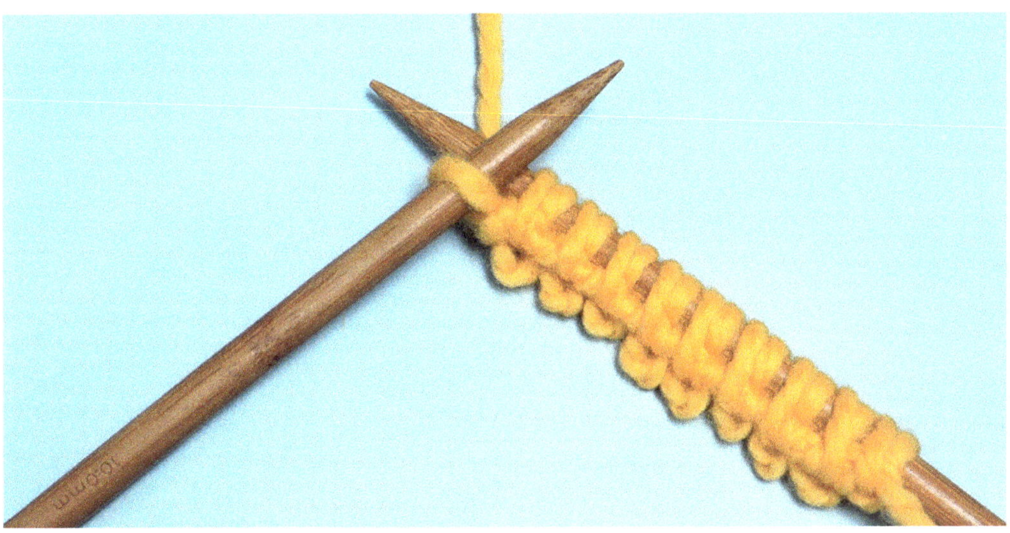

Knit the last stitch.

As you pull the yarn from under the bottom of the cast-on edge, you will notice that by the time we get to the end of the row, we've **almost doubled the number of stitches**. This is perfectly fine. We'll deal with those extra stitches in the next step.

STEP 3. ROW 2. RIGHT SIDE OF THE WORK

Now it is time to **get rid of the extra stitches** that we created in the previous step. We'll do it by knitting every two stitches together.

To ensure the stitches do not have a slant, we start by **knitting the first stitch of the row** without pairing it with its neighbour.

Then, we knit the **next two stitches** together.

And we **keep knitting every two stitches together** until we get to the very end of this row.

Now the **number of stitches is back** to the number that we cast on in step 1.

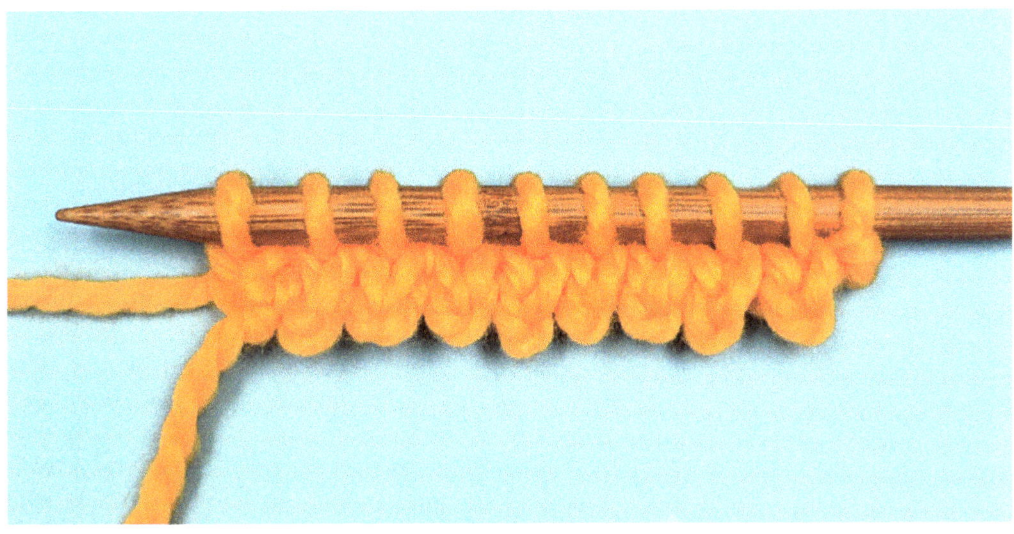

Turn the work and follow the instructions for the **first wrong-side row** of your project. Because my swatch is worked in stockinette stitch, I **purled all stitches** in the first row.

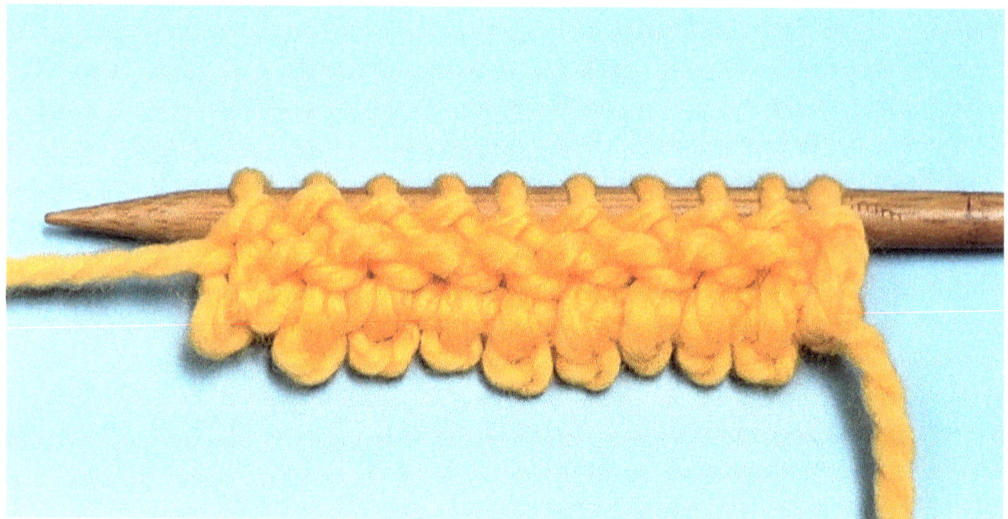

This edging looks great with any stitch pattern. It **blends in** with the smooth texture of stockinette and stockinette-based stitch patterns, and it provides **contrast to textured stitch patterns** like garter stitch.

PICOT CAST ON WORKED IN THE ROUND

When we want to add this cast on edge to a **seamless project**, we follow the same steps, but with a **few adjustments**.

STEP 1

1.1. Cast on the number of stitches that you need for your project using the **slingshot version of the long-tail cast-on method** described on pages 37-41.

1.2. Without turning the work, **arrange all stitches** for knitting in the round. I'll use double-pointed needles, but it is perfectly fine to use any other **setup that allows us to knit seamlessly**—one short circular needle, two circular needles, or one long circular needle used with the magic loop method.

Because we didn't turn the work, the first stitch that we cast on is now the **first stitch on the left needle,** and the last cast-on stitch is the first stitch on the right needle.

Make sure the stitches are **not twisted around the needle**, then **join them in a circle** as follows:

1.3. With the **yarn at the front** of the work, slip the **first cast on stitch** purlwise from the left needle to the right needle.

1.4. Insert the tip of the left needle **from left to right** into the last stitch that you cast on. It will be the **second stitch** on the right needle.

1.5. Pass that stitch **over the first stitch** from the tip of the right needle, but **don't drop that stitch**. It should now be the first stitch from the tip of the left needle.

If the last cast-on **stitch got a bit loose**, pull the working yarn and the yarn tail in the opposite directions to **tighten that stitch**.

Take an **empty needle in your right hand,** and you'll be ready to make a lovely picot edge.

STEP 2. ROUND 1

We start this round by **pulling the yarn from under the cast-on edge**. Because we don't turn the fabric when we work in the round, we'll use a **mirror version** of the process that we followed when we formed picot cast on back and forth.

2.1. With the **yarn at the front** of the work, move the right **needle down** from the back to the front of the cast on edge.

2.2. Place the working yarn **underneath the tip** of the right needle.

2.3. Move the tip of the right needle (with the yarn wrap on it) **from under the cast on edge** to the back of the work.

2.4. Purl the first stitch from the tip of the left needle.

Repeat **steps 2.1 through 2.4** until you get to the very end of the round.

Now we have **twice the number of stitches** that we cast on in step 1. It is fine. We'll get rid of the extra stitches in the next step.

STEP 3. ROUND 2

Just as we did when we added this cast on edge to a project worked back and forth, we'll **knit every two stitches of this round together**. We start with the very first pair of stitches.

Then we **knit the next pair of stitches together** and repeat this simple action to the very end of this round.

Now **the number of stitches is back** to the number that we cast on in the first step.

The cast on is finished, and we can **work on the project** according to the pattern instructions.

In the above photo, the place of join is **at the very top** of the swatch. As you see, it is **fully invisible**.

If you don't mind having a **slightly visible join** at the edge, you can cast on stitches for your seamless project **the same way** as we cast on stitches for a **project worked back and forth** (see pages 37-45) and join stitches for working in the round only after you bring the number of stitches on the needles to the number that you cast on in the first step.

When you weave in the tails, use the yarn tail to **stitch the gap** at the beginning of the round.

PICOT BIND OFF WORKED FLAT

Because the cast-on edge that we are trying to match consists of **two parts**—a double-layered edge and a set of little picots on top of each stitch—we'll have to do a few very interesting manipulations to form a **thick edge with picots** as we bind off stitches.

I've tested a handful of different solutions with mixed results before I settled on a combination of **two methods** that create a **very similar look** to the one produced by the picot cast-on method. And it is not just the look. The edges have a **similar thickness** and elasticity.

If you'd like to make the bind-off edge **more elastic**, use needles in a **bigger size**. If elasticity is not your biggest concern, the needles that you used to make your project will do just fine.

STEP 1. PREPARATION ROW

Purl all stitches in the last wrong-side row of your project.

This step is true for **all stitch patterns**. No matter what stitch pattern you use as the main pattern of your project, when you work the last wrong-side row, **purl all stitches**.

STEP 2. RIGHT SIDE OF THE WORK

In this step, we'll **form the double-layered edging** that gives the border its amazing puffy texture.

This edging is made of **two layers of stitches**. one set of stitches already sitting on our needles.

The trick is to **make a twin stitch** to each of our stitches without reorienting that stitch and without making holes between the stitches.

We'll do it by **knitting a stitch from the top part** of each stitch that is one row below every stitch on the left needle. **Here's how:**

2.1. Knit the first stitch.

2.2. With the yarn at the back of the work, insert the tip of the right needle **from front to back** under the **top part of the stitch that is below** the first stitch on the left needle.

2.3. Wrap the tip of the right needle with the yarn as we do when we **knit a stitch**.

2.4. Pull the yarn through to **form a twin stitch** to the first stitch from the tip of the left needle..

2.5. Insert the tip of the right needle **from right to left** into the first stitch on the left needle.

2.6. Take the left needle out, **slipping this stitch to the right needle**.

Repeat **steps 2.2 through 2.6** to the end of the row. By the time you finish this row, you will **almost double the number of stitches** on your needles.

It might seem a bit counterintuitive considering that this method is supposed to help us to close the stitches, not to clone them, but bear with me—**all stitches will be nicely finished off** in the next step.

STEP 3. WRONG SIDE OF THE WORK

In this step, we'll **knit every pair of stitches together,** and we'll wrap the working yarn around each stitch to **mimic the little picots** that decorate the top of the cast-on edge created by the picot cast-on method.

Here's how we do it **step by step**:

3.1. With the yarn at the back of the work, insert the tip of the right needle **from left to right** into the first pair of twin stitches on the left needle.

3.2. Wrap the tip of the right needle with the yarn and **knit these two stitches together**.

3.3. Take the working yarn in your right hand and move it **clockwise around the stitch** on the right needle—to the right, to the front, to the left, and finally, to the back of the work.

3.4. Knit the next pair of stitches together. Now we have **two stitches** on the right needle.

3.5. Pass the second stitch from the tip of the right needle over the first one and **off the needle**, the same way as we do when we bind off stitches.

Repeat **steps 3.3 through 3.5** (make a yarn wrap, knit 2 stitches together, and pass the second stitch on the right needle over the first one) until you get **to the last stitch of the row**.

Work step 3.3 **one more time** to make a yarn wrap around the stitch on the right needle. Then **knit the last stitch** and pass the second stitch from the tip of the right needle over the first one and off the needles.

Cut the yarn and **pass the yarn tail through the last stitch**. Pull tight to secure.

Whether you choose to add picot bind off to a project worked flat or the one worked in the round, the edge formed by this method will **look very similar to the edge formed by picot cast on**—the same thick edge and similar picots on top of each stitch.

PICOT BIND OFF WORKED IN THE ROUND

To add this bind-off edge to a **seamless project**, we will follow the same steps as the ones that we performed when we used this method to bind off stitches of a project worked flat, but with **one unusual twist**.

STEP 1. PREPARATION ROUND

Knit all stitches for one round.

STEP 2

In this round, we'll **form the double-layered edging**, but this time, we'll add a twin stitch **to each stitch** sitting on the needles, doubling the number of stitches by the end of the round.

We do it in **exactly the same way** as we did when we added twin stitches to the swatch worked flat. Work **steps 2.2 through 2.6** described on pages 55-57.

Repeat these steps **to the end** of the round.

Now it is time to turn the twin stitches into a textured edge while **adding yarn wraps** to decorate each bound-off stitch with a yarn picot, like a cherry on top of the cake.

STEP 3

This step starts with the **unusual manoeuvre** that I mentioned earlier—we **turn the work**.

We rarely turn the fabric to the wrong side when we work in the round, but this time, we need to do it because it is **the easiest and most efficient way** to form a picot edge **that is identical** to the edge we created when we added picot bind off to a project worked flat.

With the **wrong side of the fabric facing you**, bring the **yarn to the back** of the work.

You can turn the project inside out, or you can simply **rotate the work** so that the beginning of the round is at the **side that is farther from you**, as I did to the swatch shown in the photo below.

Work **steps 3.1 through 3.5** described on pages 58-60.

Repeat **steps 3.3 through 3.5** (pages 59-60) to the very end of the round.

When you have one stitch left on the right needle, **work step 3.3 again** to wrap the last stitch clockwise with the yarn.

Cut the yarn, leaving a **tail around 20 cm / 8" long**. Pass this tail through the last stitch, being careful not to lose the yarn wrap.

Pull the tail to **tighten the last stitch** while turning the yarn wrap into the last picot bead.

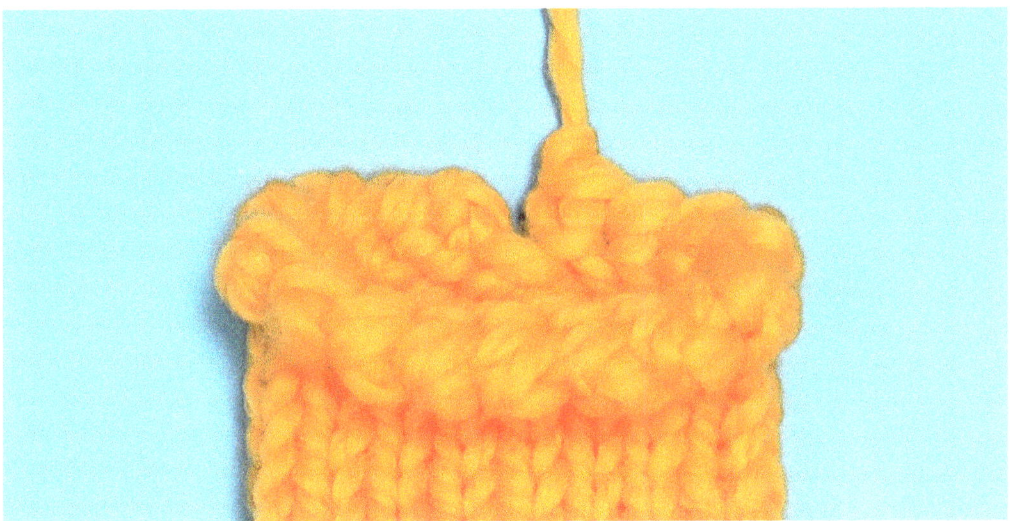

The stitches are finished off and the edge looks great. But because we **turned the work** at the beginning of step 3, **there is a gap** between the first and the last bound-off stitches.

We'll easily fix this gap with **one overhand stitch**.

Here's how we do it:

Thread the yarn tail into a wool needle and place the project so that the **wrong side of the gap is facing you**.

Insert the wool needle **from left to right** under the left-leaning strand at the **very bottom of the picot** on top of the first stitch **at the left side** of the gap.

Then insert the wool needle **from left to right** under the strand that is at the **very bottom of the picot** on top of the first stitch **at the right side** of the gap.

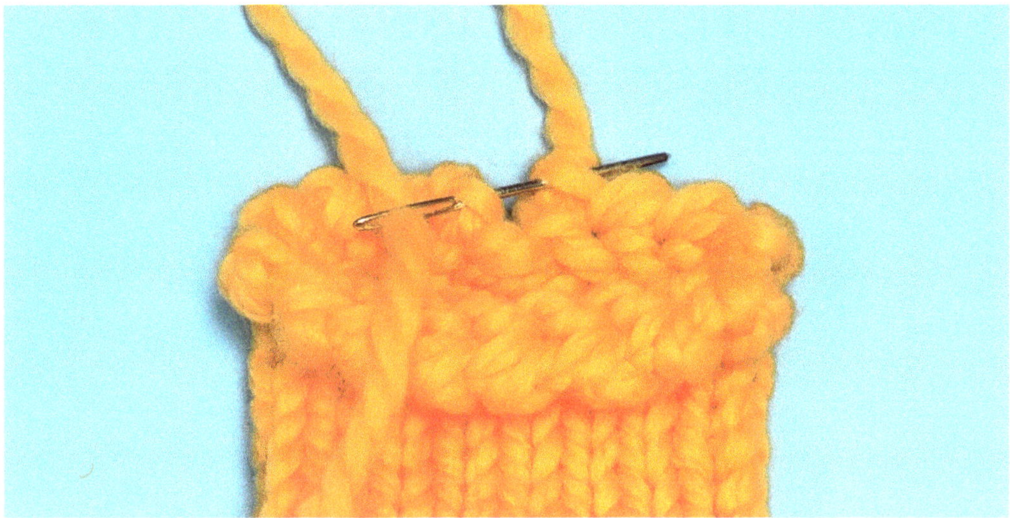

Pull the yarn through, **joining the ends of the bind-off edge** in a clean, invisible way. Secure the yarn tail and hide it within the bind-off edge.

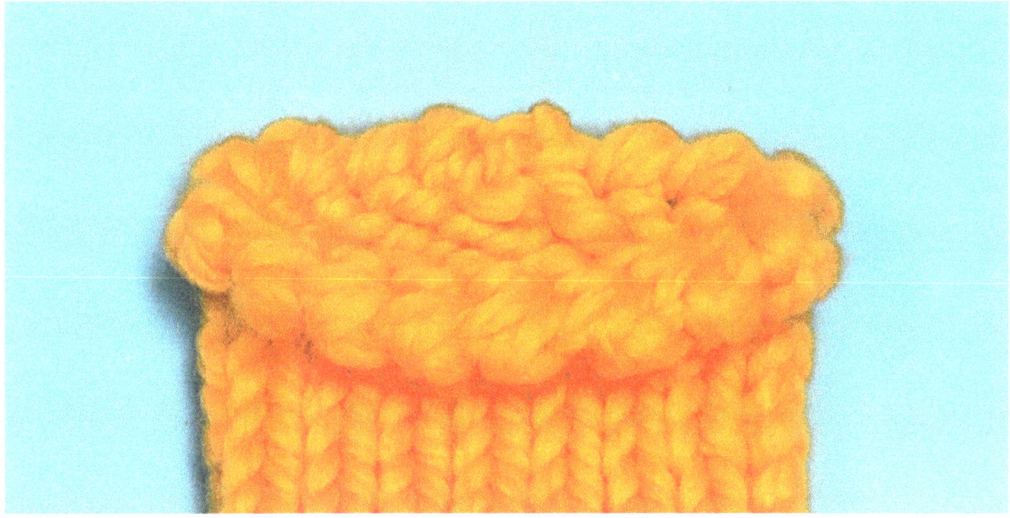

We've just formed a beautiful picot edge that looks **exactly the same** as the picot **edge worked back and forth** and is **almost identical** to the edge formed by the **picot cast-on** method.

CRISS-CROSS CAST ON AND CRISS-CROSS BIND OFF

STRETCH ★★★☆☆

DIFFICULTY ★★★★☆

TOOLS

Let's use some elements of the picot edging that we've just learnt and make an **elaborate border** that has a good amount of stretch but also **holds its shape well.**

Decorated with a **set of long crossed stitches**, this border will add a beautiful detail to any project. And of course, we'll make sure the borders we form at the cast-on and the bind-off edges are **very similar**.

CRISS-CROSS CAST ON WORKED FLAT

Cast on **any number of stitches** using the slingshot version of the **long-tail cast on** described on pages 37-41. To make my test swatch, I cast on 10 stitches.

ROW 1. RIGHT SIDE OF THE WORK

1.1. Knit one stitch.

1.2. Pull the yarn **from under the cast on edge** the same way as we did when we made picot cast on worked flat (see steps 2.2 through 2.4 described on pages 42-43)—move the tip of the **right needle down** and to the back of the cast on edge, **wrap the working yarn** around the tip of the right needle the same way as we do when we knit a stitch, and move the tip of the right needle (with the wrap on it) **from under the cast on edge** to the front of the work.

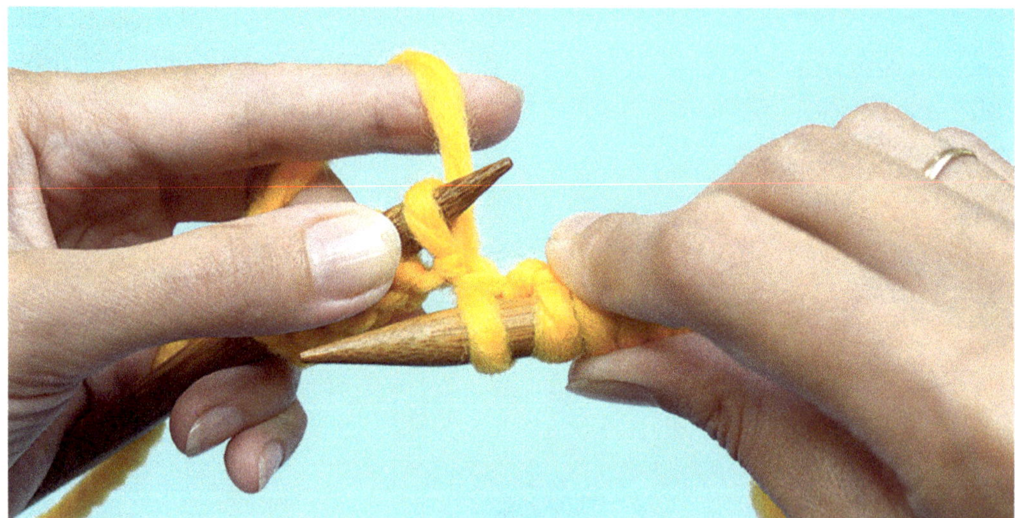

Repeat steps 1.1 and 1.2 until you get **to the last stitch** of this row. Knit the last stitch.

The number of stitches on the needles **almost doubled**, but we already know that it is not a big deal. We'll turn these stitches into a beautiful textured edge **in the third row** of the pattern, but first, let's make the edge even thicker and even more textured.

ROW 2. WRONG SIDE OF THE WORK

To create that additional texture, we are going to knit the stitches that we cast on, and we'll **slip the stitches that we added** by pulling the yarn from around the cast-on edge.

2.1. Knit one stitch.

2.2. Bring the **yarn to the front** of the work and **slip one stitch purlwise** from the left needle to the right needle.

Repeat steps 2.1 and 2.2 **to the last stitch** of the row. Knit the last stitch.

Be careful not to mix up stitches. It is important that we knit the stitches that we cast on and slip the pulled stitches that we created in the previous row.

ROW 3. RIGHT SIDE OF THE WORK

This is the row when we finally **bring the number of stitches back** to the number that we cast on. We'll do it by turning the pulled stitches into beautiful crosses that make this border so interesting.

3.1. Knit one stitch.

3.2. Knit two stitches together **through the back loop**. The first of these two stitches should be a pulled stitch that we formed in the first row and slipped in the previous row.

Repeat step 3.2 **to the end of this row** to knit every pair of stitches together through the back loop.

ROW 4. WRONG SIDE OF THE WORK

This row is super simple—we **knit all stitches** one by one. This is how we form a ridge that separates this border from the main fabric of the project.

The border is finished, and we can **work in the main pattern** of the project, starting with a right-side row.

To highlight the unusual texture of this edging, I made my swatch in stockinette stitch, but **it will look lovely with any stitch pattern** you choose to use.

CRISS-CROSS CAST ON WORKED IN THE ROUND

The elasticity of this edging makes it perfect for hats, mittens, top-down cottage socks and other seamless projects.

To make the edge look the same around the whole circumference of the project, it is important to **avoid interrupting the pattern**. Not an easy task with an elaborate border like criss-cross edging.

We'll make it happen by working **four rounds**, using **a few tricks** that will guarantee the border is consistent and that it looks exactly the same as the criss-cross edging formed when we work flat.

We start by using the slingshot version of the **long-tail cast on** (see pages 37-41) to cast on **any number of stitches**.

Without turning the work, arrange the stitches for working in the round.

I'll make my swatch on **five double-pointed needles**, so I divided 16 stitches that I cast on into four equal groups and slipped each group to a separate needle.

You can also use **any other way to work in the round**—one short circular needle, two circular needles, or one long circular needle used with the magic loop method.

Because we didn't turn the work, the **last stitch that we cast on** is now the **first stitch** from the tip of the needle **at the right side** of the gap.

Make sure the **stitches are not twisted** around the needles, then bring the **yarn to the back** of the work and **join stitches in a circle** by passing the last cast-on stitch over the first one without dropping either of these stitches (see **steps 1.3 through 1.5** on pages 48-49).

ROUND 1

This round is very **similar to row 1** of the instructions that explain how to make this edging back and forth.

1.1. Knit 1 stitch.

1.2. Make a stitch by **pulling the yarn from around the cast-on edge** (see steps 2.2–2.4 on pages 42-43).

Repeat **steps 1.1 and 1.2 to the end** of this round.

We **doubled the number of stitches** in this round, but it is totally fine—we'll turn these extra stitches into a beautiful line of crossed strands in the third round of the pattern.

ROUND 2

2.1. Purl 1 stitch.

2.2. Bring the **yarn to the back** of the work, and **slip 1 stitch purlwise** from the left needle to the right needle.

Repeat **steps 2.1 and 2.2 to the end** of this round.

ROUND 3

This round is crucial for forming the lovely line of crossed strands and for ensuring this line goes around the edge uninterrupted.

To achieve the flow of the pattern, we'll use an interesting concept known as the **"travelling stitch"**. It is occasionally used in lace patterns worked in the round, and it helps to keep the pattern consistent.

In a nutshell, the travelling stitch means **shifting the beginning of the round by one stitch** to avoid a jog or other disruptions to the pattern.

To make the shift more obvious, I will use a stitch marker in my swatch.

If you don't use a marker in your project, there is **no need to add it to the work**—simply slip the first stitch from the left needle to the right needle, and remember that the beginning of the round is going to shift in this round.

If you work with one circular needle, then you are likely using the stitch marker already. In this case, follow the instructions below to a tee.

With the **yarn at the back** of the work, remove the marker.

Slip 1 stitch purlwise to the right needle and **place the marker** on the right needle.

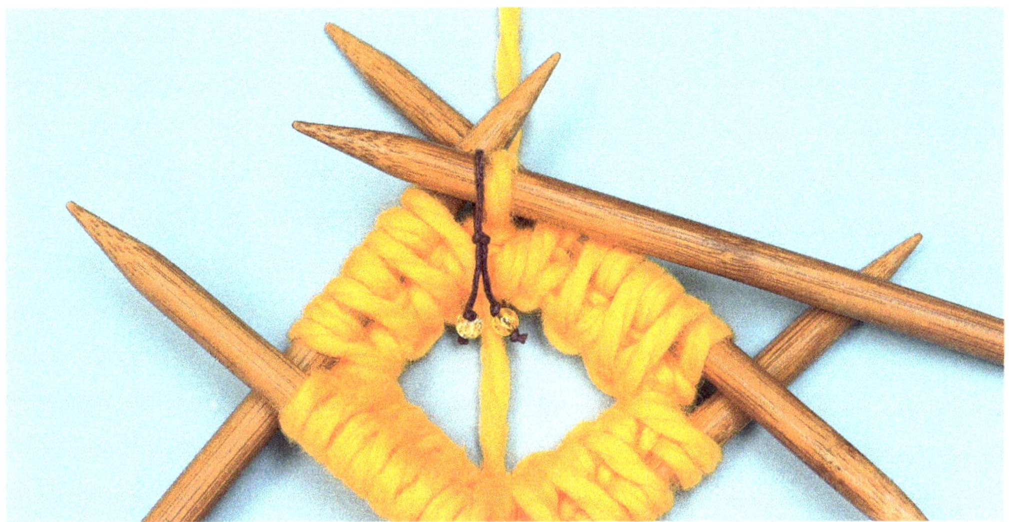

3.1. Knit two stitches together **through the back loop**.

Repeat step 3.1 to **knit every two stitches together** through the back loop to the end of the round.

As you knit two stitches together, make sure **the pulled stitch formed in round 1 is the first one** from the tip of the left needle.

Now we are **back to the number of stitches** that we cast on.

If you use **double-pointed needles**, you will shift stitches by one stitch every time you move to another needle. It could be a bit uncomfortable, but don't worry—we won't do it again after we finish this round.

This "stitch shifting" is **the only way to make the pattern consistent**, so it is definitely worth the effort. As you see in the photo below, the line of crossed strands is **not interrupted** at the beginning of the round.

ROUND 4

The task of the last round is to **highlight the beautiful texture** of this edging and to **separate it** from the main pattern of the project.

This round is the easiest of the four—we simply **purl every stitch** of the round.

Now the edging is finished, and we can **work in the main pattern** of the project.

There is **no need to shift the beginning of the round back** by one stitch to the "true" beginning of the round. It is easier to accept the "shifted" beginning of the round and use it as you work in any stitch pattern of your choice.

CRISS-CROSS BIND OFF WORKED FLAT

We start to make this edging with a wrong-side row, so before you work row 1 described below, **make sure you are looking at the wrong side of the work** and the working yarn is at the right side of the project.

ROW 1. WRONG SIDE OF THE WORK

Knit all stitches.

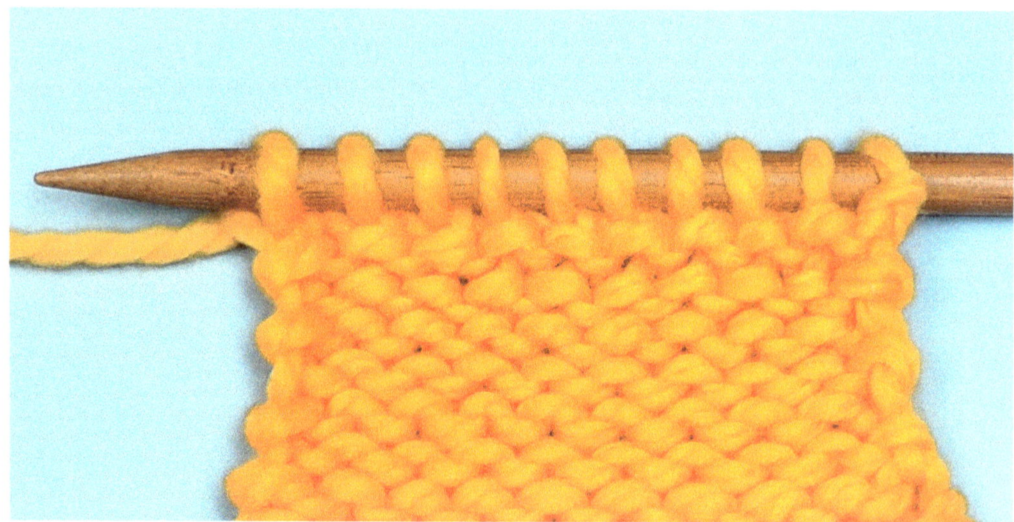

We need this row to **visually separate the edging** from the rest of the project.

ROW 2. RIGHT SIDE OF THE WORK

In this row, we'll add more stitches to the work so that the **total number of stitches almost doubles**. These extra stitches will later form the lovely criss-cross pattern. They will also make the edge thicker and more stable, so that it could **keep the fabric from curling** even when most of the project is worked in stockinette stitch.

To add those helpful stitches to the project, we'll use a **slightly unusual way** that is explained in step-by-step photos below.

2.1. Insert the tip of the right needle **from front to back** into the space between the first two stitches on the left needle.

2.2. Wrap the needle with the working yarn as we do **when we knit** a stitch.

2.3. Pull the wrap through the fabric to form a new stitch.

Make this new stitch **fairly loose** if you want to create a puffier texture with a more vivid criss-cross pattern.

2.4. Knit one stitch.

Repeat steps 2.1 through 2.4 until you get **to the last stitch of this row**. Knit the last stitch.

ROW 3. WRONG SIDE OF THE WORK

It is a **preparation row** for shaping the criss-cross pattern. To make sure the stitches form vivid elongated X's, we need to **twist and slip each stitch** that we added in the previous row.

Here's how we do it **step by step**:

3.1. Knit one stitch.

This is the **odd stitch** that didn't get a companion new stitch in the previous row. This stitch is not included in the pattern repeat. It is destined to be lonely in this row.

3.2. Knit one stitch.

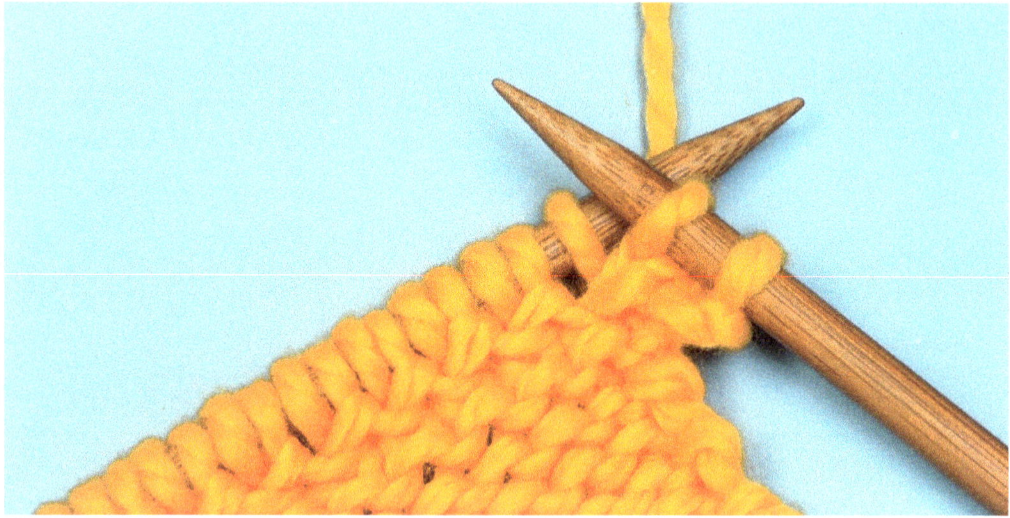

Make sure this is **one of the "resident" stitches,** not a stitch that we created in the previous row.

3.3. Bring the **yarn to the front** of the work and insert the tip of the right needle from left to right **under the back leg** of the first stitch on the left needle. This should be a **stitch formed from a yarn wrap** in row 2.

Ease the left needle out, slipping this stitch to the right needle.

Repeat steps 3.2 through 3.3 **to the end** of the row.

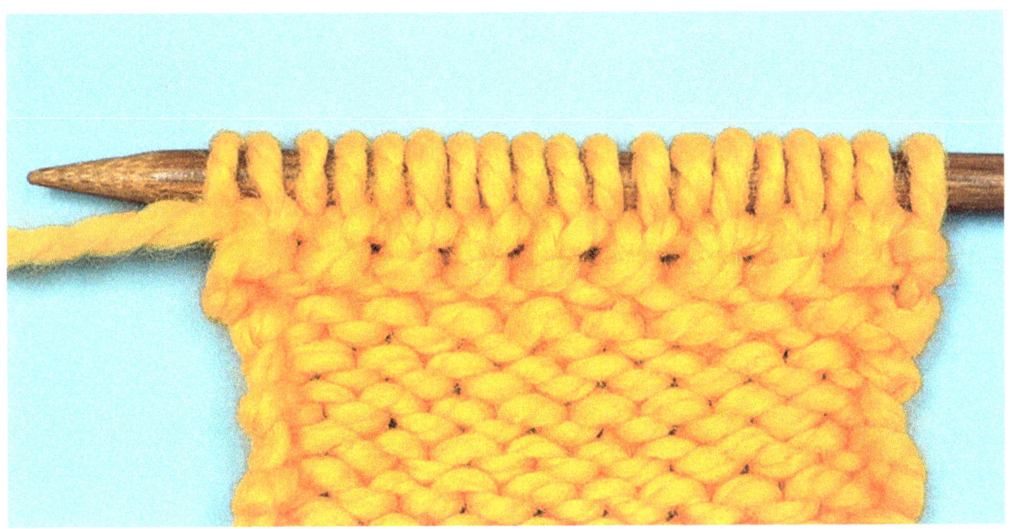

ROW 4. RIGHT SIDE OF THE WORK

The previous two rows set the scene for the criss-cross edging. Now we are **ready to make a beautiful line of crossed strands**, bring the number of stitches back to the original number, and bind off all stitches while forming a line of knots at the top of the bind-off edge.

We'll accomplish all these tasks **in the same row**. Here's how:

4.1. Knit two stitches together **through the back loop**.

Make sure **the first of the stitches is a long pulled stitch** added to the work in row 2 and slipped with a twist in row 3.

4.2. Take the working yarn in your right hand and **move it clockwise around the stitch** on the right needle—to the right, to the front, to the left, and finally to the back of the work. For better results, keep this wrap **fairly loose**.

We used this trick to make picots on top of the edge formed by the picot bind-off method. This time, we use it again to create the **knot-like look** that is similar to the one that we see at the very bottom of the criss-cross cast-on border.

4.3. Knit the next two stitches together **through the back loop**.

Now we have **two stitches** on the right needle.

4.4. Pass the second stitch from the tip of the right needle over the first one the same way **as we do when we bind off** stitches.

Repeat steps 4.2 through 4.4 until you get **to the last stitch** of the row.

Work **step 4.2 one more time** wrapping the stitch with the yarn, then knit the last stitch **through the back loop**.

Bind it off by passing the second stitch from the tip of the right needle over the first one.

Wrap the last stitch with the yarn **as we did when we worked step 4.2.**

Cut the yarn and thread the yarn tail through the last stitch, being careful **not to lose the last wrap**. Pull the tail tight to secure the yarn, and hide it within the edging.

As you see, this bind-off edge looks **very similar to the criss-cross cast on edging**.

If you use this cast-on + bind-off pair on a scarf or a blanket, your project will have edges that not only match but **also look great on both sides** of the work and **keep the fabric from curling**.

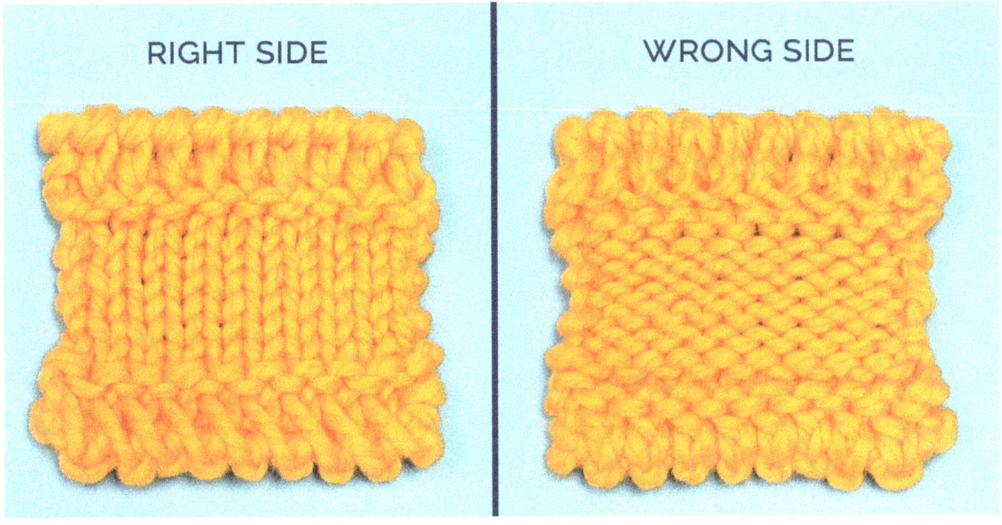

CRISS-CROSS BING OFF WORKED IN THE ROUND

When we want to use this bind-off edging to finish a top-down hat, a cowl, or any other seamless project, we need to **make a few adjustments** to the process that we followed when we added this edging to a project worked flat.

ROUND 1

Purl all stitches.

ROUND 2

Make a new stitch the same way as we did in steps 2.1 through 2.3 described on pages 87-88, then **knit one stitch**.

Repeat this sequence of making one stitch and knitting one stitch to the end of the round.

ROUND 3

With the yarn at the back of the work, insert the tip of the right needle from left to right into the **back loop of the first stitch** from the tip of the left needle. It will be the extra stitch created in the previous step.

Take the left needle out to **slip this stitch** to the right needle.

Bring the **yarn to the front** of the work and purl the next stitch.

Repeat these steps **to the end** of the round.

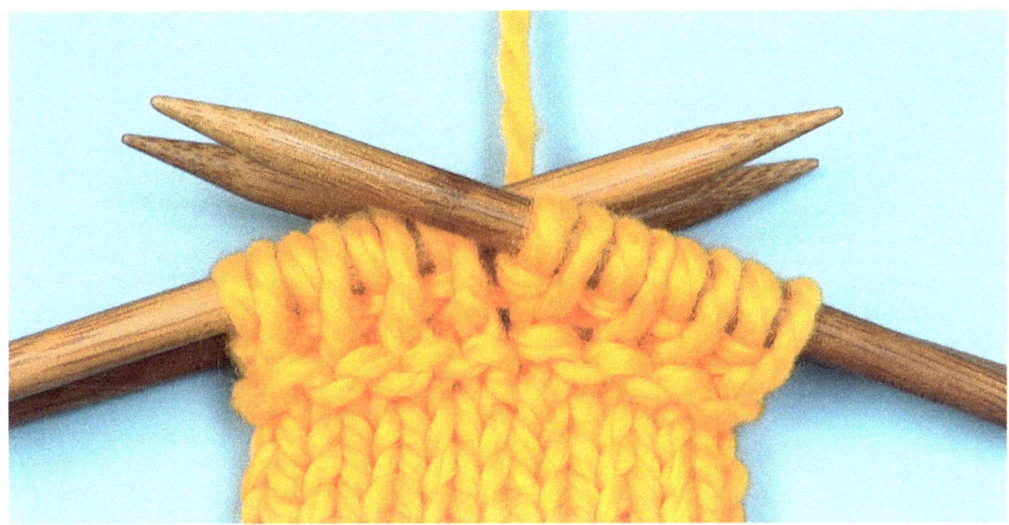

ROUND 4

In this round, we'll make **the same wraps** as we made in the last row of this edging worked flat.

Because we need to pass the yarn around the right needle, it is **more convenient to use a double-pointed needle** as your right-hand needle.

Work steps 4.1 through 4.4, described on pages 92-93, then repeat **steps 4.2 through 4.4 to the end** of the round.

Work **step 4.2 one more time** to wrap the last stitch with the yarn. Cut the yarn, leaving a tail around 15 cm / 6" long. Pass the tail through the last stitch and pull tight to secure.

The last thing we need to do is to **fix the gap** between the first and last bound-off stitches. It is easier to do it on the wrong side of the work.

Rotate the work so that the **wrong side of the gap is facing you** and insert the yarn tail into a wool needle.

Insert the wool needle **from right to left** under the edge strand at the bottom of the first knot-like yarn wrap at the right-hand side of the gap, and **from right to left** under the strand at the bottom of the last bound-off stitch.

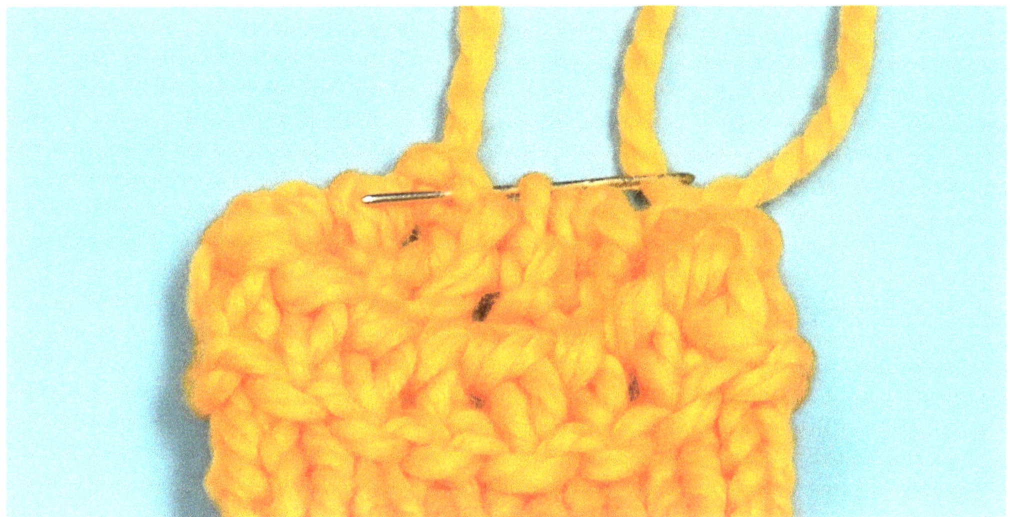

Pull the yarn through, closing the gap in a **neat, invisible way**.

Secure the yarn and **hide the yarn tail** within the edging.

Now you can add this lovely bind-off edging **to any project**, no matter whether it is **worked flat or in the round**.

DOUBLE-CHAIN CAST ON

Use a crochet hook that is **two sizes smaller** than the needles.

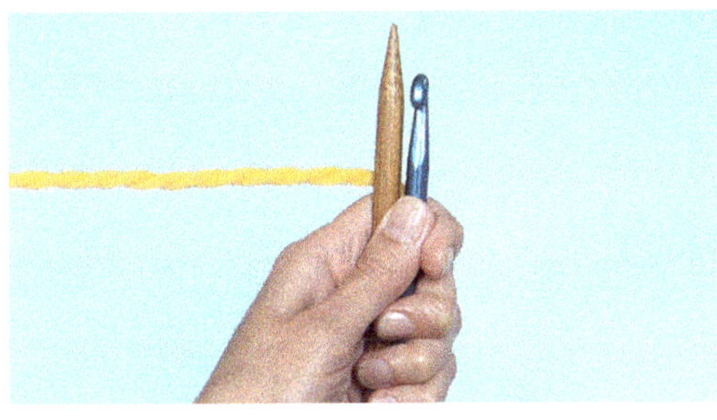

Place the yarn at the back of the aligned needle and crochet hook, and hold it all in your left hand.

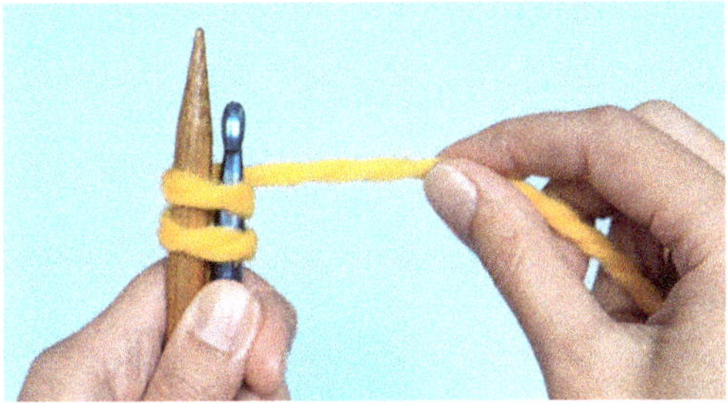

Wrap the yarn twice around both tools from the back, to the right, to the front, and to the back again.

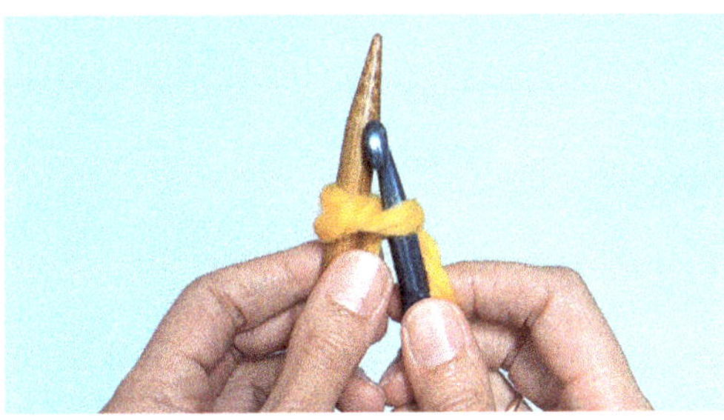

With the hook, pull the second wrap through the first one. Next time, pull it through the wrap and the stitch sitting on the hook.

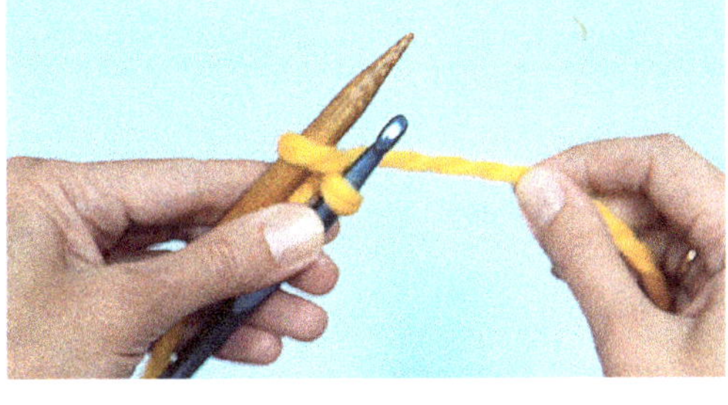

Undo a part of the second wrap by moving the yarn to the front and through the slot between the needle and the head of the hook.

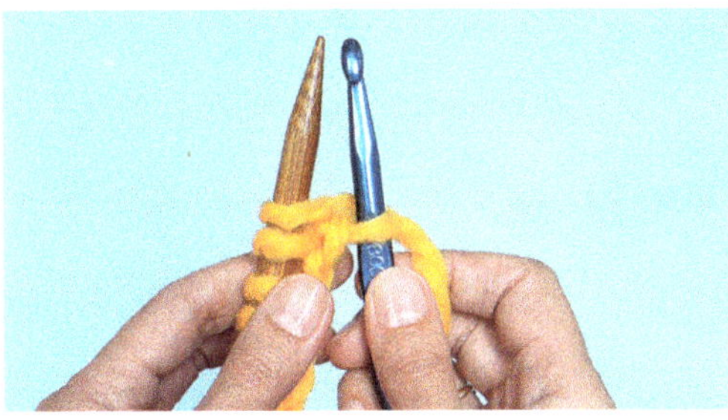

Repeat until the needle holds the number of stitches that you need minus one stitch.

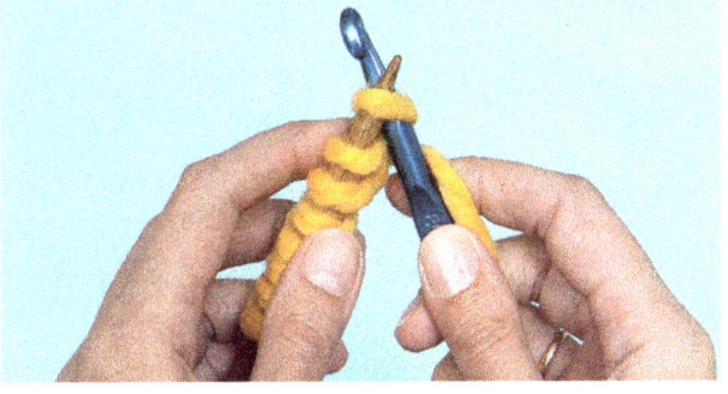

Slip the last stitch knitwise from the crochet hook to the knitting needle.

DOUBLE-CHAIN BIND OFF

With the right side facing you, bring the yarn to the front of the work.

STEP 1. Eastern purl. Insert the right needle into a stitch, place the yarn underneath the tip of the needle, and pull it through.

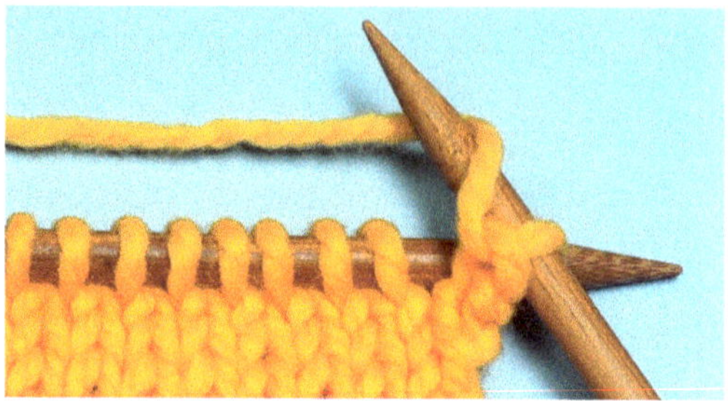

STEP 2. Make a regular yarn over, then move the yarn to the front of the work.

STEP 3. Purl the next stitch using the Eastern method described in step 1.

STEP 4. Bind off the yarn over by passing it over the first stitch and off the right needle..

STEP 5. Pass the second stitch on the right needle over the first one and off the needle.

Repeat steps 2 through 5 until you bind off all stitches. Then cut the yarn and secure the yarn tail.

PICOT CAST ON

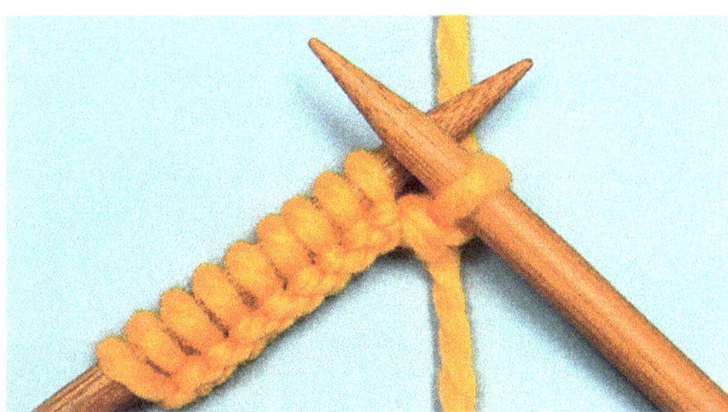

Use long-tail cast on to cast on the number of stitches you need. **STEP 1.** Knit one stitch.

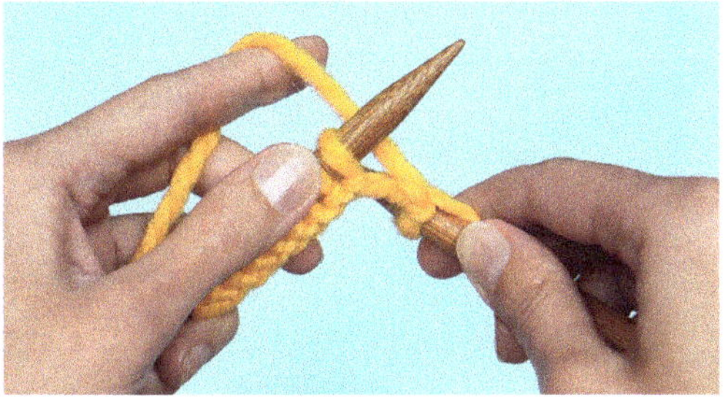

STEP 2. Move the tip of the right needle down and to the back of the cast-on edge.

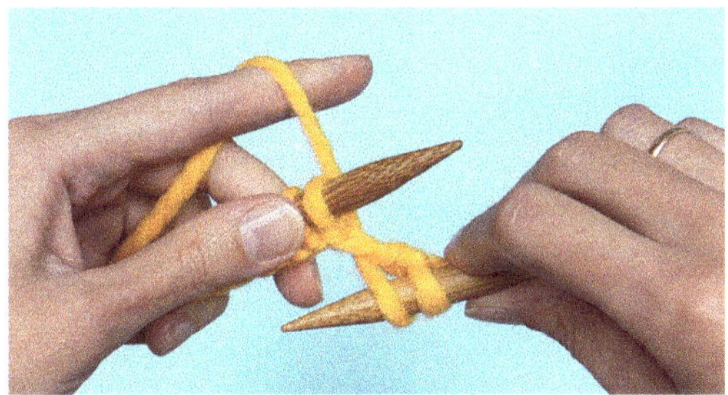

STEP 3. Wrap the needle with the yarn as we do when we knit a stitch, and move it from under the edge to the front of the work.

Repeat steps 1 through 3 to the last stitch. Knit the last stitch and turn the work.

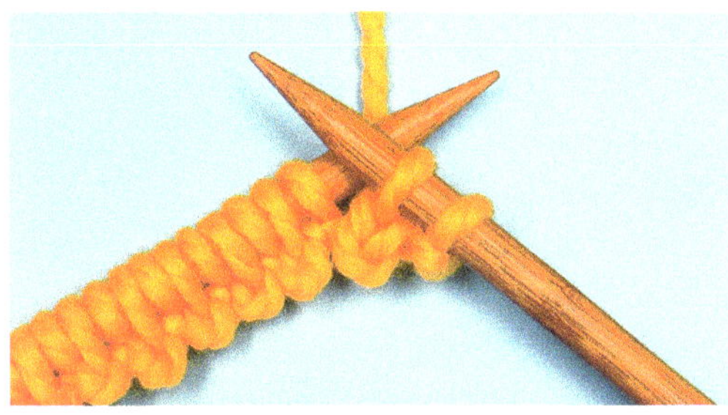

Knit the first stitch, then knit the next two stitches together.

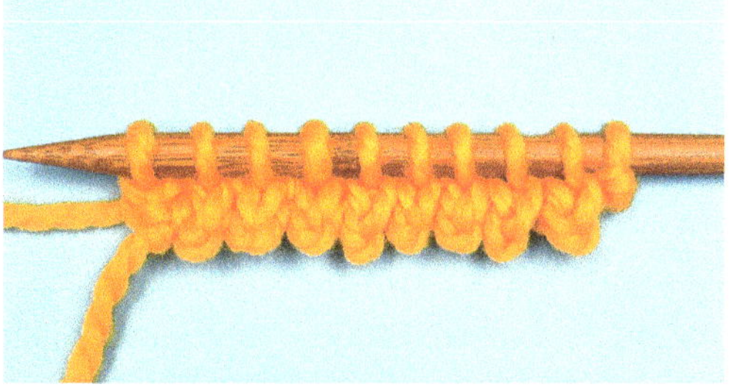

Keep knitting every two stitches together to the end of the row.

Turn the work and make the first wrong-side row of your project.

PICOT BIND OFF

Knit 1 stitch. **1.** With yarn at back, insert right needle from front to back under top part of the stitch below first stitch on left needle.

2. Wrap the needle with the yarn as we do when we knit a stitch, and pull this wrap through to make a "twin" stitch.

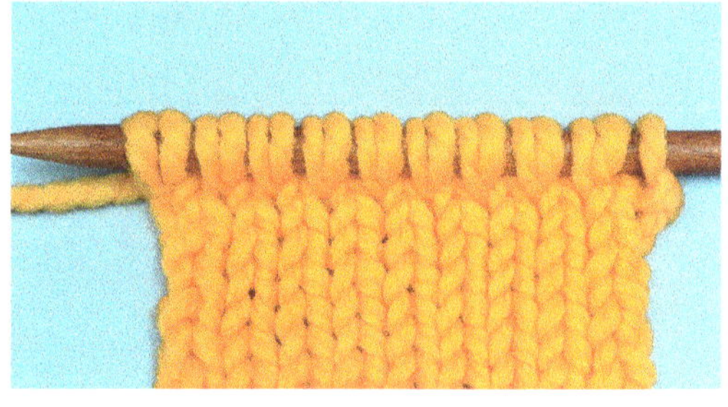

3. Slip 1 stitch purlwise from the left needle to the right needle.

Repeat steps 1 through 3 to the end of the row. Turn the work.

Knit 2 stitches together. **4.** Wrap the resulting stitch with the yarn clockwise—to the right, to the front, to the left, and to the back.

5. Knit the next pair of stitches together. **6.** Pass the second stitch on the right needle over the first one and off the needle.

Repeat steps 4 through 6 to the end of the row.

CRISS-CROSS CAST ON

PART 1

Cast on any number of stitches using a slingshot version of the long-tail cast on.

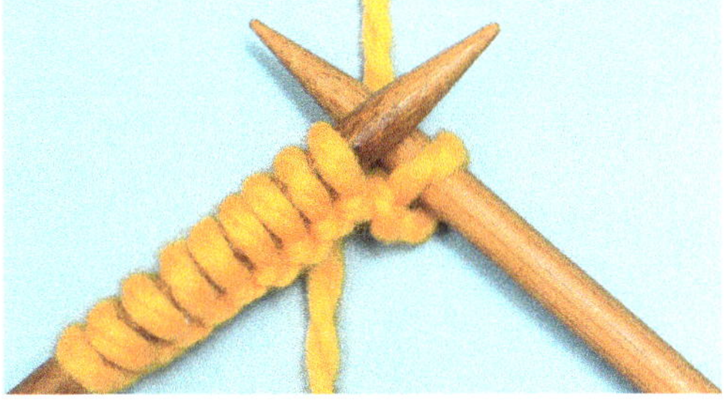

ROW 1.

STEP 1.1. Knit 1 stitch.

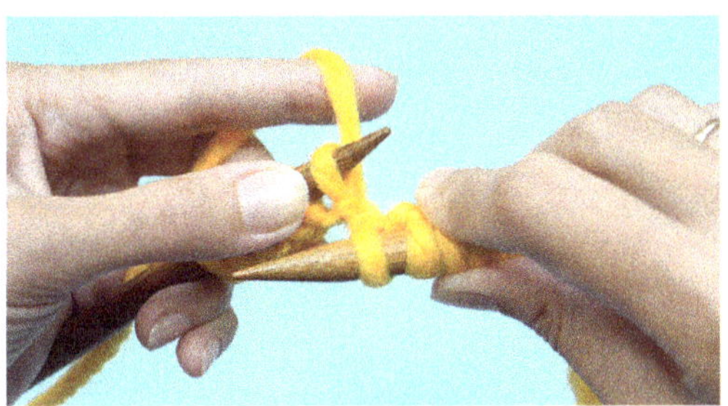

STEP 1.2. Make 1 stitch by pulling the yarn from under the cast-on edge.

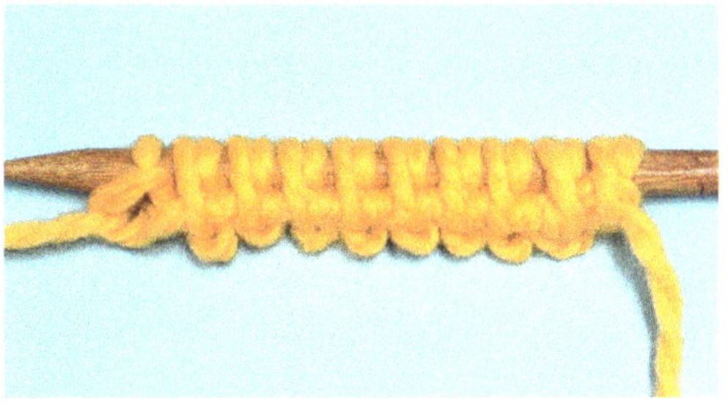

Repeat steps 1.1 and 1.2 to the last stitch of the row. Knit the last stitch.

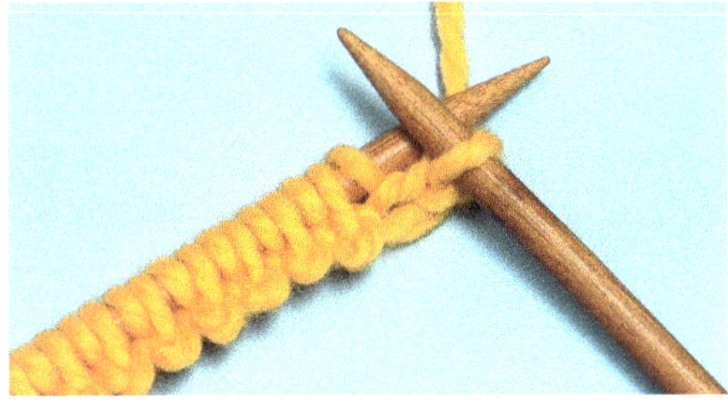

ROW 2.

STEP 2.1. Knit 1 stitch.

STEP 2.2. Slip 1 stitch purlwise with the yarn in front. It should be a "pulled" stitch formed in step 1.2.

CRISS-CROSS CAST ON

PART 2

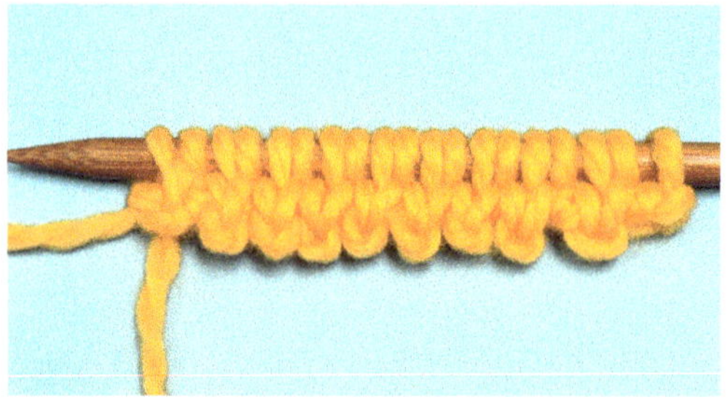

Repeat steps 2.1 and 2.2 to the last stitch of the row. Knit the last stitch.

ROW 3.

STEP 3.1. Knit 1 stitch.

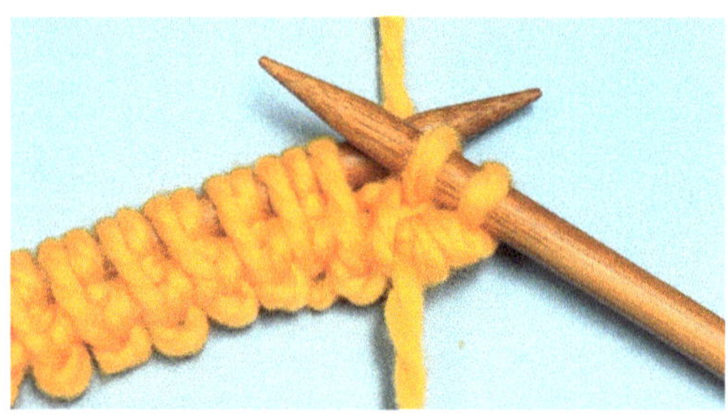

STEP 3.2. Knit 2 stitches together through the back loop. The first one should be a "pulled" stitch.

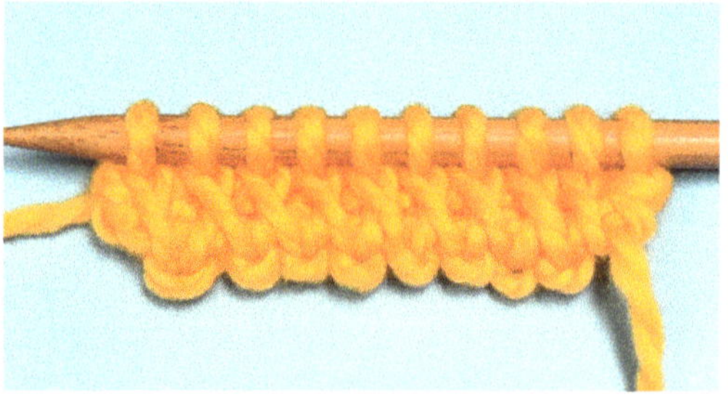

Repeat step 3.2 to the end of the row.

ROW 4. Knit all stitches one by one.

Work in the main pattern of the project, starting with a right-side row.

CRISS-CROSS BIND OFF

PART 1

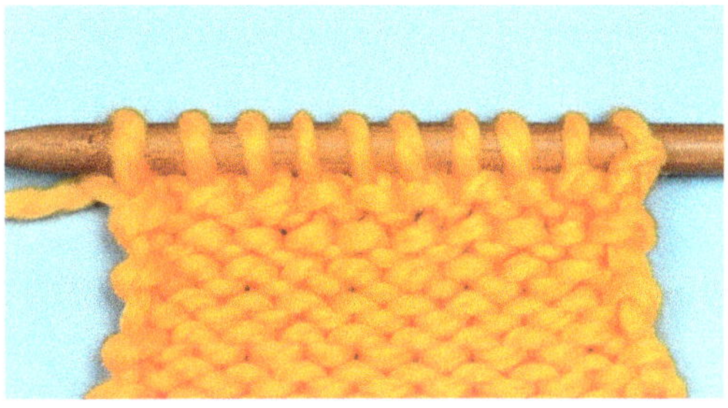

ROW 1. With the wrong side of the fabric facing you, knit all stitches.

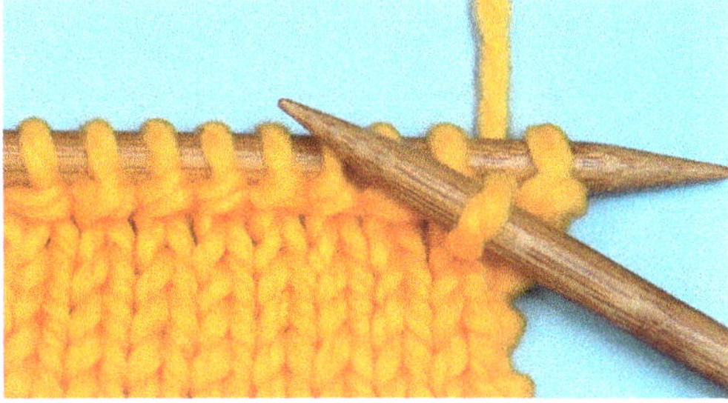

ROW 2. STEP 2.1. Make 1 stitch by pulling the yarn from the space between the first two stitches on the left needle.

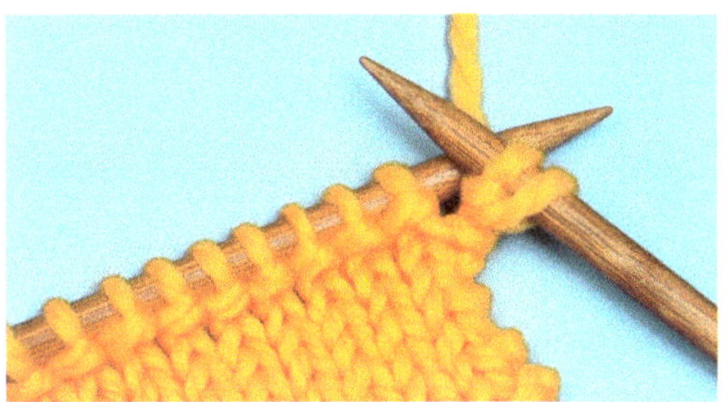

STEP 2.2. Knit 1 stitch.

Repeat steps 2.1 and 2.2 to the last stitch. Knit the last stitch.

ROW 3. Knit one stitch.

STEP 3.1. Knit one stitch.

STEP 3.2. With yarn in front, insert the right needle left to right under the back leg of the next stitch.

CRISS-CROSS BIND OFF

PART 2

STEP 3.3. Slip this stitch to the right needle. This should be a stitch formed in step 2.1.

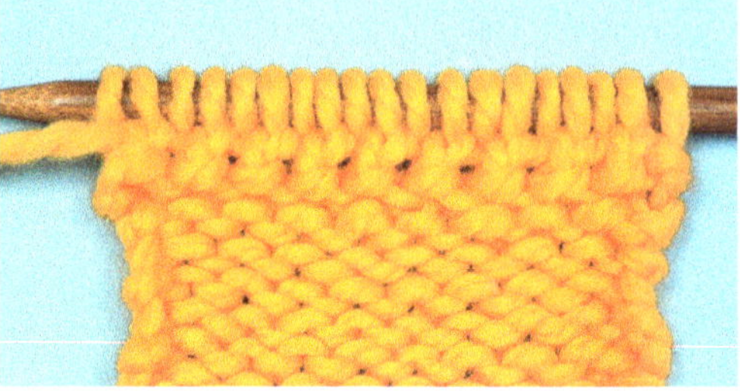

Repeat steps 3.1 through 3.3 to the end of the row.

ROW 4. Knit 2 stitches together through the back loop. First stitch should be the one formed in 2.1.

STEP 4.1. Move the yarn clockwise around the stitch on the right needle.

STEP 4.2. Knit 2 stitches together through the back loop. **STEP 4.3.** Bind off 1 stitch.

Repeat steps 4.1 through 4.3 to the end of the row. Cut the yarn and pull it through the last stitch.

INVISIBLE EDGES

TUBULAR CAST ON AND BIND OFF FOR 1X1 RIBBING

STRETCH ★★★★★

DIFFICULTY ★★★☆☆

TOOLS

When I first started to knit sweaters, I wanted them to look **exactly like store-bought garments**.

At that time, "handmade" was **almost synonymous with "unprofessional"** and even "low quality". Of course, I didn't want that for my sweaters, so I tried to avoid the "handmade look" as much as I could.

I used fine yarn and thin needles. I spent hours fixing mistakes, even the ones that no one would ever notice, but there was one thing that invariably gave me away—a **stiff ridge at the bottom** of the sweater and the cuffs.

The bottom band and the cuffs were usually knitted in **1x1 ribbing**, and because I used "good old" long-tail cast on (the only type of cast on I knew back then), there was always a ridge at the bottom edge.

That ridge not only looked unprofessional, but it also **restricted the elasticity** of the fabric.

And then I **discovered tubular cast on** (also called *the long-tail tubular cast on* in some sources). This way to cast on stitches is a game-changer. It creates a **beautifully elastic cast-on edge**, is perfect for 1x1 ribbing, and doesn't form a ridge at the bottom. The best part—it is also quite easy to do.

TUBULAR CAST ON FOR 1X1 RIBBING WORKED FLAT

First, let's see how we can add this edge to scarves, blankets, and other **projects worked back and forth.**

STEP 1

Leave a tail that is **at least four times as long as** the length of the cast-on edge. Place the tail on your left thumb and the working yarn on your left index finger.

Hold both strands with the other three fingers of your left hand, just as we do when we cast on stitches using the long-tail cast-on method.

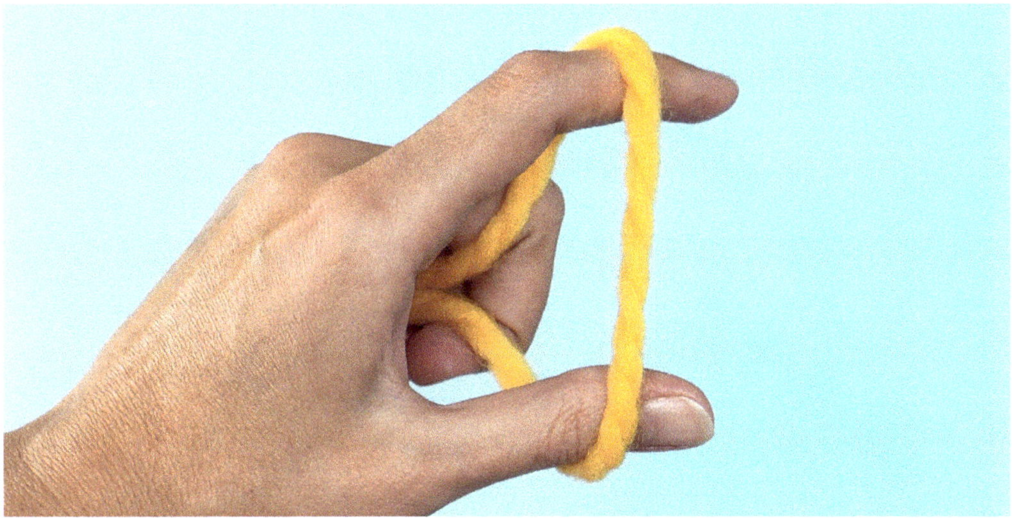

|STEP 2

Take a knitting needle in your right hand and **place it on top** of the strand stretched between your left thumb and your index finger.

Move the needle down and to the right to **create a loop by twisting the yarn**. This loop is our first stitch.

Note that the yarn should be twisted in such a way that the strand that comes from the thumb (the yarn tail) **is at the front** of the strand that comes from the index finger (the working yarn).

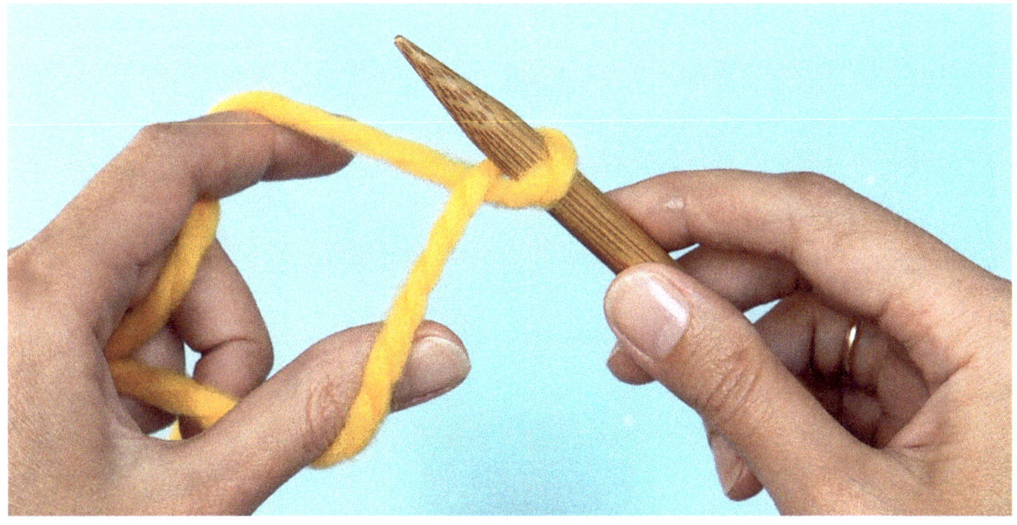

STEP 3

With the tip of the needle, **pick the working yarn** from right to left.

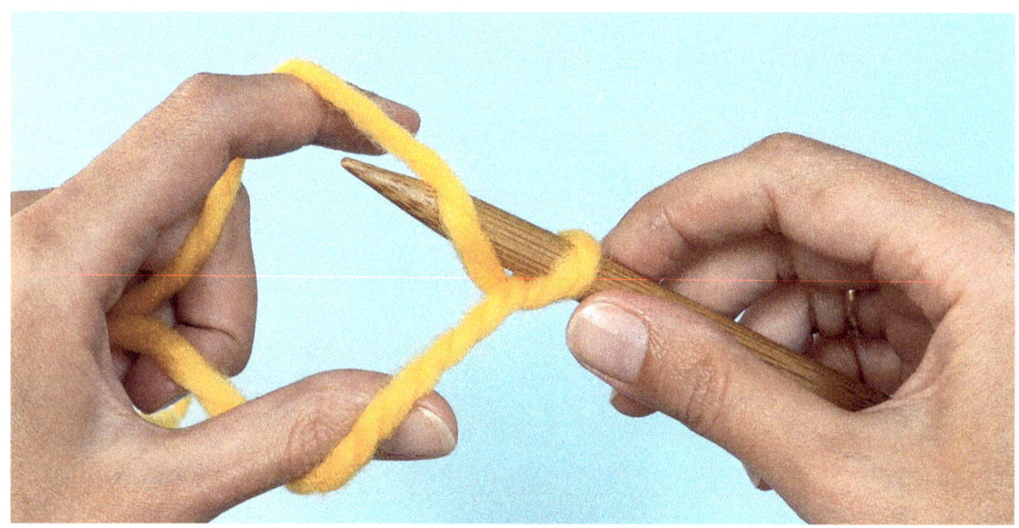

Then **pick the yarn tail** from the bottom up.

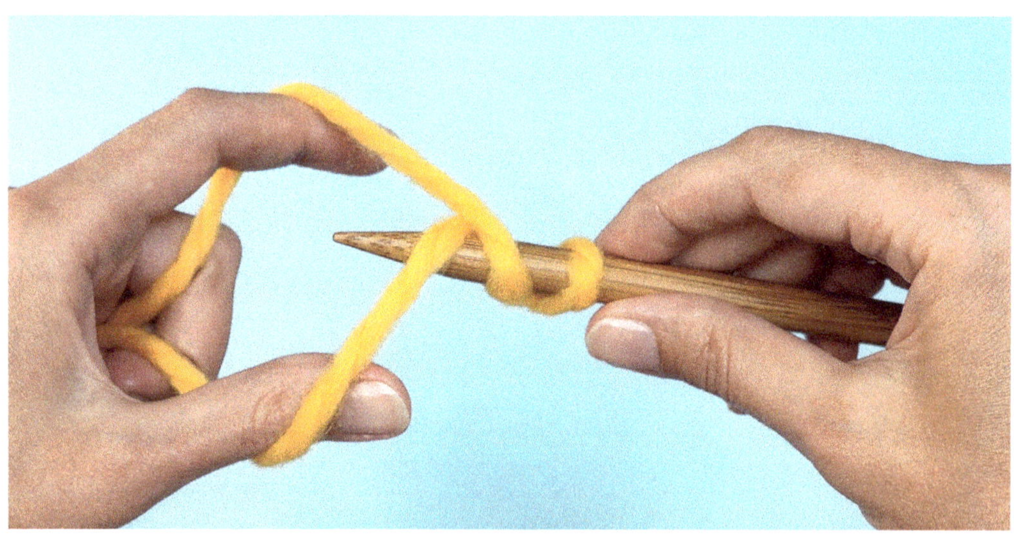

Finally, move the needle **from under the working yarn,** forming a new stitch.

As you can tell from the **horizontal bar at the bottom** of the new stitch, we've just **created a purl** stitch.

STEP 4

This step is very similar to the previous step, but we'll start to make a new stitch **from the other side.**

First, **pick the yarn tail** from the bottom up.

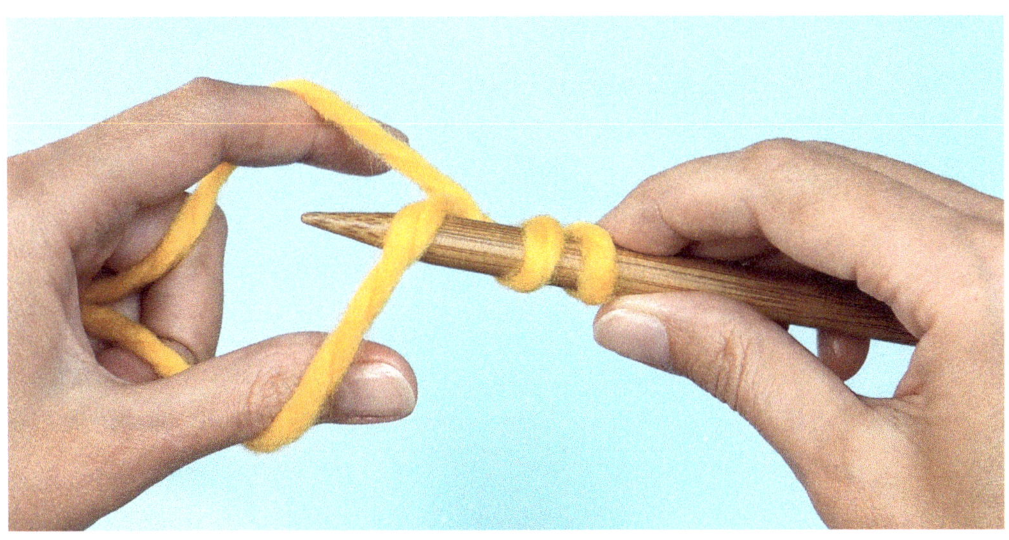

Then, **pick the working yarn** from right to left.

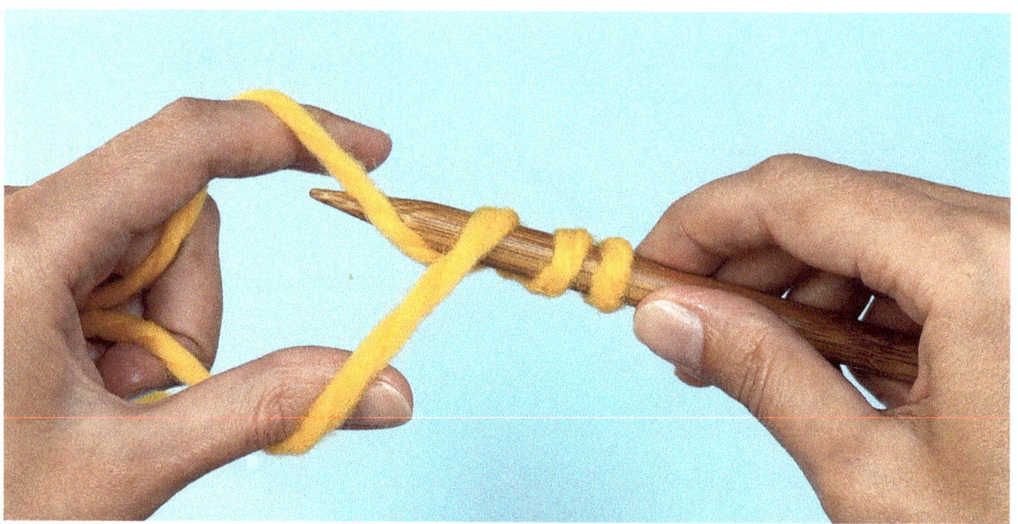

Finally, move the tip of the needle **from under the yarn tail**.

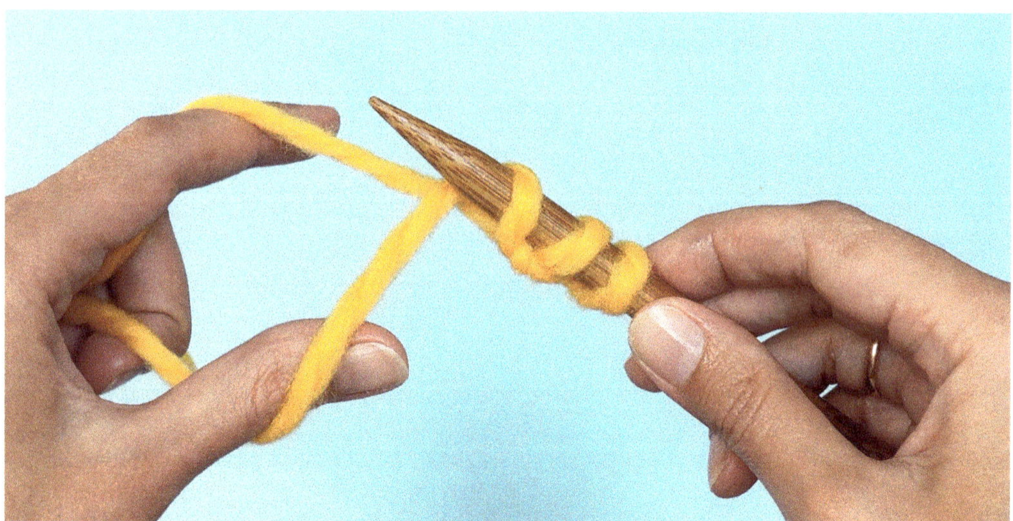

Because we started from the other strand, **this step resulted in a new knit stitch**.

Repeat steps 3 and 4 to **cast on as many stitches as you need** for your project. If the ribbing starts with a knit stitch (as it usually does), and you need to cast on an even number of stitches, finish casting on after you make a purl stitch in step 3.

Keep the newly cast-on stitches **quite snug** to give the edge a nice polished look. If you tend to form loose stitches, use a **needle in a smaller size** when you cast on stitches.

If you stop or get distracted while you cast on stitches and you can't remember which way to go to cast on the next stitch, **look at the twist** at the bottom of the needle. To cast on the next stitch, go under the strand that is at the back of the twist, then pick the strand that is at the front of the twist.

When you finish to cast on stitches, twist the working yarn and the yarn tail **at the very bottom of the last stitch**. Then turn the work, being careful not to undo the final twist.

FIRST ROWS

With this type of cast on, getting the initial set of stitches on the needle is **only half the task**. The way we work the first rows is also important. These rows are meant to set up the pattern and to ensure that the edge is consistent and neat.

There are **two main ways to work the first rows**, each of the ways creating a slightly different edge.

WAY 1. ITALIAN CAST ON

This way is **the easier** of the two—simply **work in the "knit 1, purl 1"** ribbing pattern, knitting every knit stitch through the back loop.

If you cast on an **even number of stitches**, the first row will look like this:

SETUP ROW

Knit 1 stitch through the back loop, purl 1 stitch.

Repeat this sequence to the end of the row.

If you have an **odd number of stitches** on the needles, **purl the first stitch**, and then work the sequence described above.

Starting with row 2 of the project, work in the established ribbing pattern.

This method is often called the **Italian cast on** and it is a variation of the "true" tubular cast on.

The *Italian* edge is thinner, a bit more elastic, and it **tends to flare out**.

WAY 2. "TRUE" TUBULAR CAST ON

When we use this method, we **slip all purl stitches** in the first two rows of the project. Those slipped stitches **form a tube** that gives this method its name.

This tube **makes the edge fuller**, highlighting the effect of the fabric flowing around the edge. It also keeps the edge from stretching out.

If you cast on an **even number of stitches**, the first two rows will be worked as follows:

SETUP ROW 1

Knit 1 stitch **through the back loop**, then bring the **yarn to the front** of the work and slip 1 stitch purlwise from the left needle to the right needle.

Make sure the **slipped stitch has a horizontal bar** at the bottom that tells us that this stitch is a purl.

Repeat this sequence **to the last two stitches** of the row, then knit 1 stitch through the back loop and **purl the last stitch**.

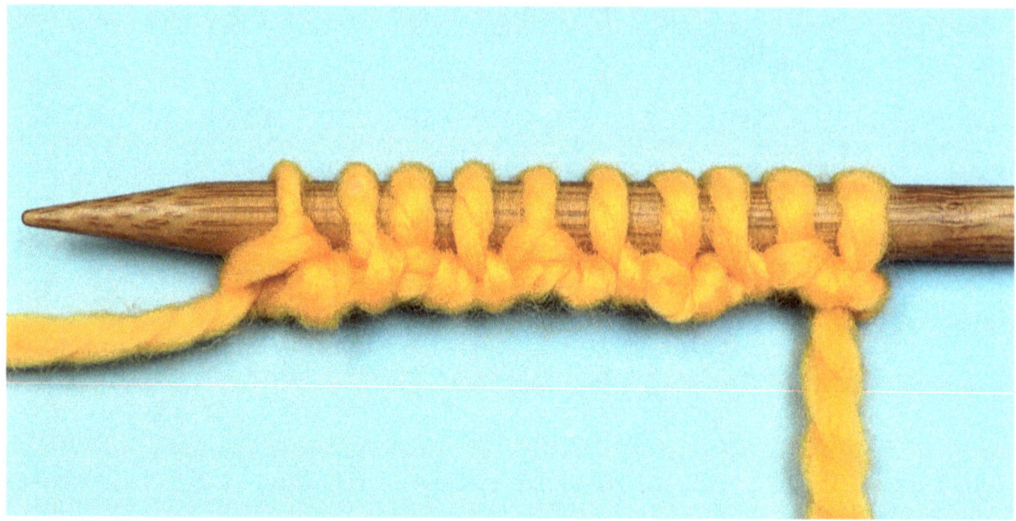

If you cast on an **odd number of stitches**, you should **slip the first stitch** of this row with the yarn in front of the work. Then repeat the sequence described above.

SETUP ROW 2

Knit 1 stitch as usual, **through the front loop**. Bring the **yarn to the front** of the work and slip 1 stitch purlwise from the left needle to the right needle.

Repeat this sequence **to the last two stitches** of the row, then knit 1 stitch and **purl the last stitch**.

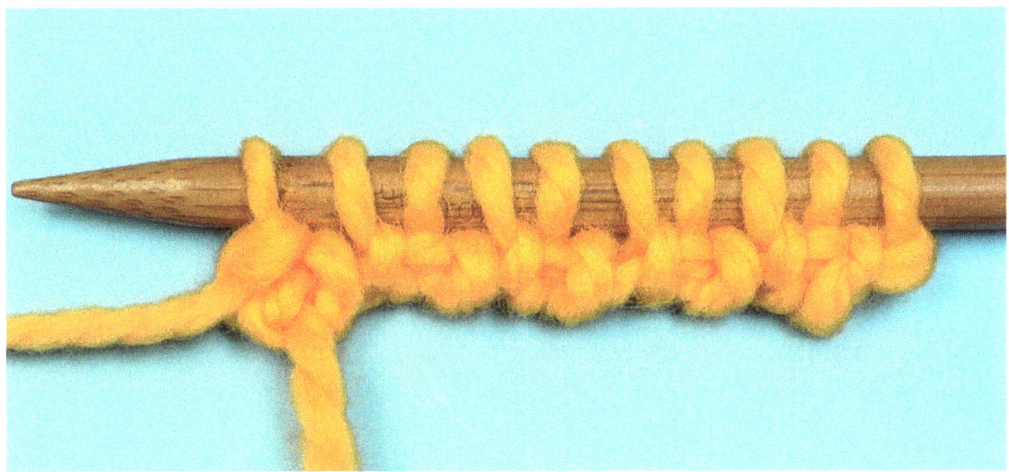

If you work with an **odd number of stitches**, repeat this sequence to the last stitch of the row, then knit the last stitch.

The cast-on edge is now formed, and we can work in the classic 1x1 ribbing pattern.

Both methods have their pros and cons, but the truth is—the result is **not *that* much different**. If you are not too fussy about the look and the elasticity of the cast on edge, **use the easier way** whenever you decide to add an invisible cast on edge to projects worked in "knit 1, purl 1" ribbing.

TUBULAR CAST ON FOR 1X1 RIBBING WORKED IN THE ROUND

The elasticity and the well-finished look of an edge formed by the tubular cast-on method make it **perfect for hats, top-down socks, mittens** and other seamless projects. But how do we make this edge when we work in the round?

Technically, it is possible to join stitches for working in the round **right after we get the initial set of stitches** on the needles. I did it a few times, and I can say that it is doable. But it is an **extremely tedious task** with a high risk of twisting the cast on edge.

There is a **much easier way** to get the same nice-looking stretchy cast-on edge without the pain of moving fragile yarn wraps between needles.

We simply make the cast on edge **back and forth** and join stitches for working in the round only after we make setup rows.

Here's how this process works step by step.

STEP 1. CAST ON

To cast on the initial number of stitches, work **steps 1 through 4** described on pages 112-116., then **repeat steps 3 and 4** (pages 114-116) until you have as many stitches as you need for your project.

Because 1x1 ribbing is worked on an even number of stitches, finish casting on stitches **after you make a purl stitch** in step 3.

Twist the working yarn and the tail at the very bottom of the last stitch, then **turn your work**.

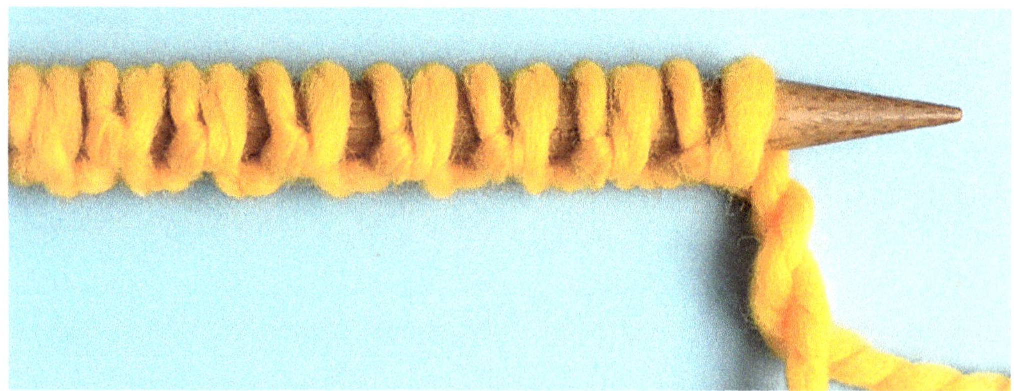

That's right—we are not knitting in the round yet. To make it **easier fo rus to arrange stitches** for working in the round, we'll first work the setup rows.

STEP 2. SETUP ROWS

If you **don't plan to add an extra texture** to the edge, and you are not worried that the edge might stretch out, work one setup row described on page 118, but **for a more professional look**, it is better to work two setup rows outlined on pages 119-121.

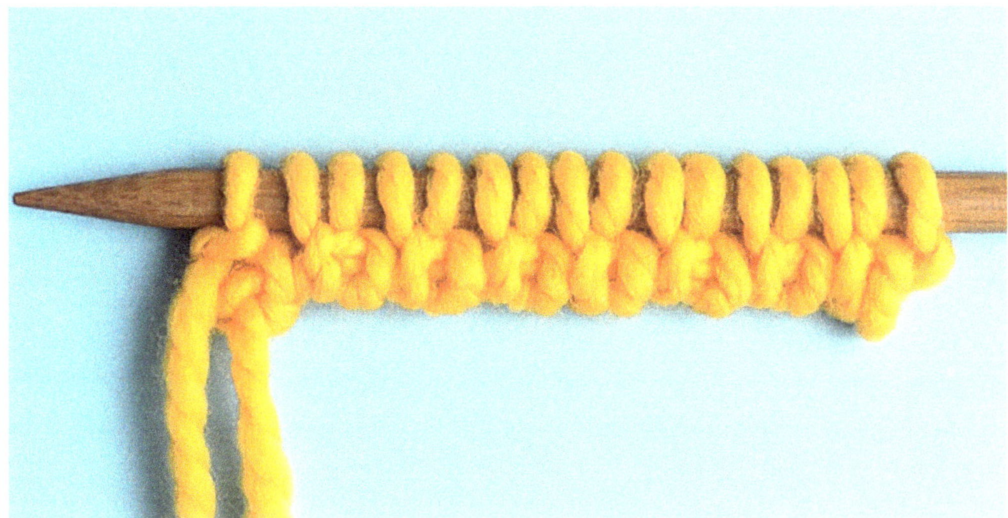

Now the stitches are not the flimsy wraps that they used to be right after we cast them on. **Setup rows gave them some body,** and now we can confidently make them ready for seamless knitting.

STEP 3. JOINING STITCHES FOR WORKING IN THE ROUND

Feel free to use double-pointed needles, one short circular needle, two circular needles, or one long circular needle and the magic loop method.

Depending on the tools you choose, **divide all stitches** between double-pointed needles, spread them on one short circular needle, or split them in half for working on two circular needles or on one long circular needle used with the magic loop method.

Make sure the cast-on **edge is not twisted** around the needles and the working **yarn is at the right-hand side** of the work.

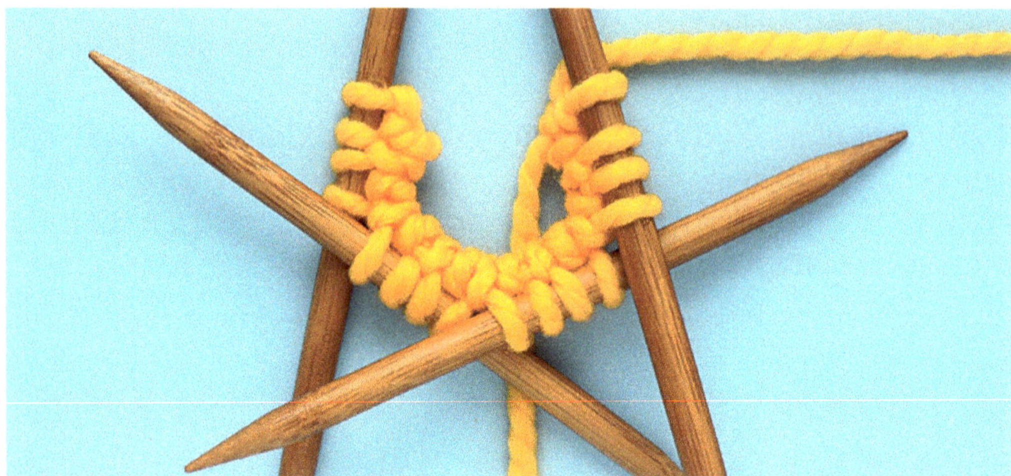

That's it—we are all set to work in the round. To make sure the pattern is consistent, **don't use any special method to join stitches** in a circle. Simply alternate knit and purl stitches to the end of each round to form a neat 1x1 ribbing.

After a few rounds, you will see that your project has a **beautiful stretchy edge.**

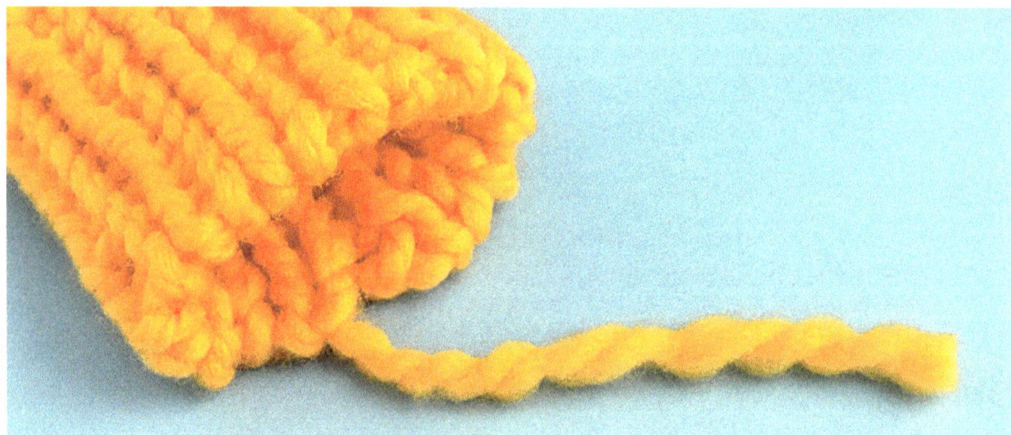

There is only **one imperfection**—the spot where we joined stitches. The setup rows formed a one-row long fabric, and even though this one row is fairly small, it does create a **tiny gap in the place of join**.

This gap is **easy to fix** with two overhand stitches. You can do it after you work a few rounds or when you weave in the yarn tails.

STEP 4. CLOSING THE GAP

4.1. Thread the yarn tail that is at the cast-on edge into a wool needle. With the right side of the work facing you, insert the wool needle **from back to front** under the strand that **forms the corner** at the right-hand side of the gap.

Pull the yarn through.

4.2. Now fold the edge so that you can **see the wrong side of the fabric**.

With the wrong side of the work facing you, insert the wool needle **from right to left** under the left leg of the first stitch at the right-hand side of the gap, and from right to left under the right leg of the first stitch at the left-hand side of the gap.

Pull the yarn through, secure it, and **hide the yarn tail** inside the edge.

These two overhand stitches do not just close the gap. They **completely conceal the spot** where the stitches were joined. No one will ever know that we used the easy way of making a tubular cast-on edge in the round.

TUBULAR BIND OFF FOR 1X1 RIBBING WORKED FLAT

To form this beautiful elastic edge when we bind off stitches, we'll **join stitches in pairs** using a wool needle.

To simplify the process, we'll take advantage of the basic fact that the stitches that we see as **purls on the right side** of the fabric look like **knits on the wrong side** of the fabric.

Instead of trying to remember a way to join knit stitches and a way to join purl stitches, we'll **alternate joining knit stitches** on the right side of the work with joining knit stitches on the wrong side of the work.

As we do that, we'll **always work stitches in pairs**, inserting the wool needle **from front to back** into the first stitch we join and **from back to front** into the second stitch.

The other thing to keep in mind is that we need to **work each stitch twice**.

But before we close the stitches, we want to make sure the bind-off edge is well-rounded and **doesn't have an inclination to stretch out** when we start to wear our precious knitted creation.

That's when preparation rows come into play.

PREPARATION ROWS

This part is **optional**. You can follow the instructions in the "Bind Off Itself" part right away, but preparation rows give the bind-off edge a **more polished look** and help the edge to keep its shape better.

These rows are very **similar to the setup rows** that we made when we used the tubular cast-on method (see page 112).

We simply knit the knit stitches and **slip the purls** with the yarn in front of the work.

PREPARATION ROW 1

Knit 1 stitch, bring the **yarn to the front** of the work, and slip 1 stitch purlwise to the right needle.

Repeat this sequence to the last two stitches of the row, then knit 1 stitch and **purl the last stitch.**

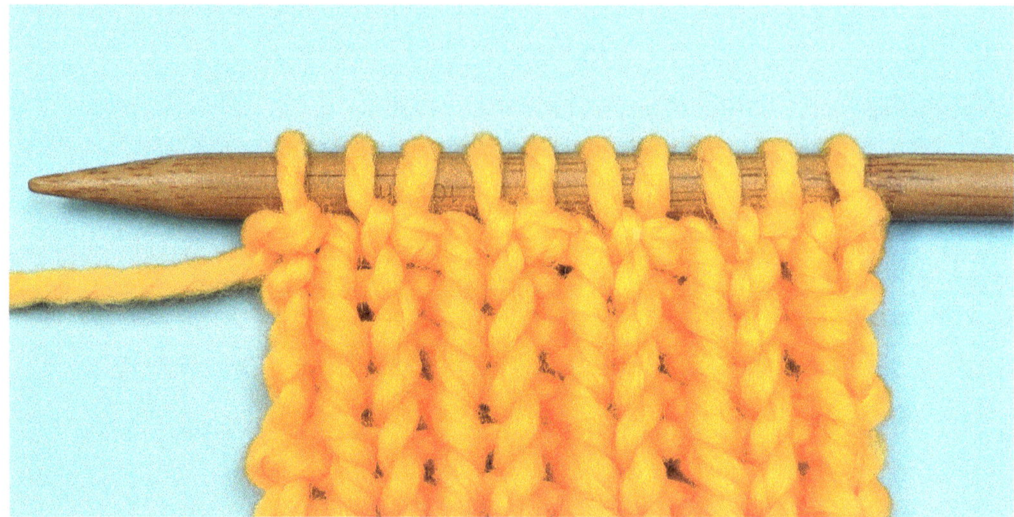

If you have an **odd number of stitches**, repeat this sequence to the last stitch of the row, then knit the last stitch. If your row starts with a purl stitch, purl that stitch, and then repeat the sequence described above.

PREPARATION ROW 2

Nothing special happens in this row. We simply repeat the same **"knit the knits and slip the purls"** process that we followed in preparation row 1.

When we get to the last stitch of the row, we purl that stitch.

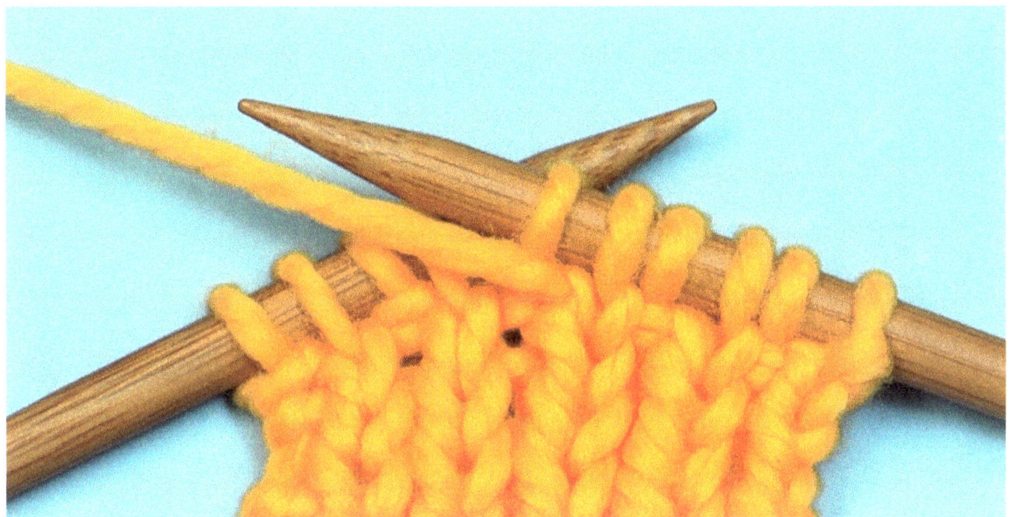

As a result, the fabric underneath the needle looks very similar to 1×1 ribbing, but it is **not quite ribbing**.

When we look closely, we'll see strands in front of purl stitches in the top row. These strands make the edge more rounded, and they also keep the fabric from stretching out.

BIND OFF ITSELF

Cut the yarn, leaving a yarn tail that is at least three times as long as the bind-off edge. Thread this tail into a wool needle.

To make it easier for you to see every strand of the seam, I will use a piece of yarn **in a different colour** as my yarn tail.

STEP 1

The first step is a bit tricky, but **it is essential** to ensure that the right-hand side of the edge is nicely shaped.

Because in most cases 1x1 ribbing starts with a knit stitch, we'll assume that **the first stitch on your needles is a knit**.

Place the wool needle **at the back of the first knit** stitch, and then insert it from left to right into the first purl stitch.

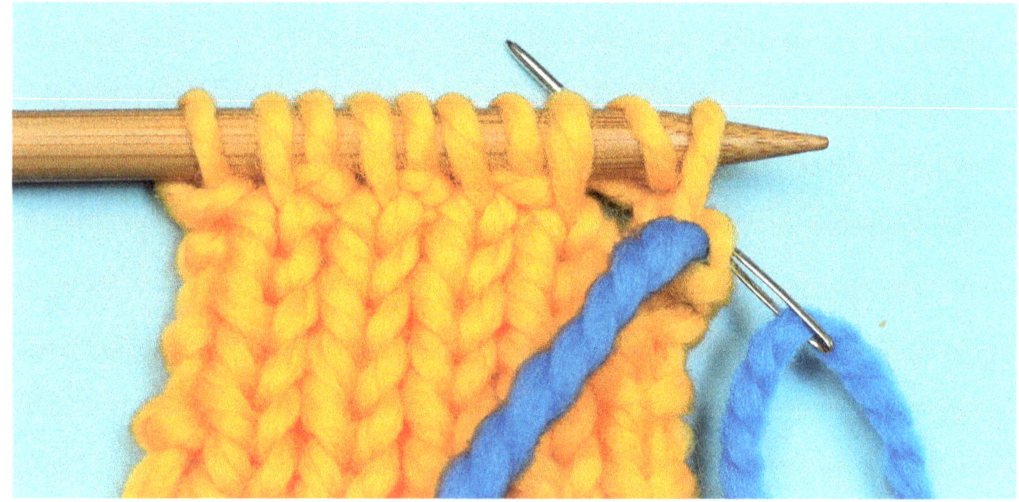

Pull the yarn through.

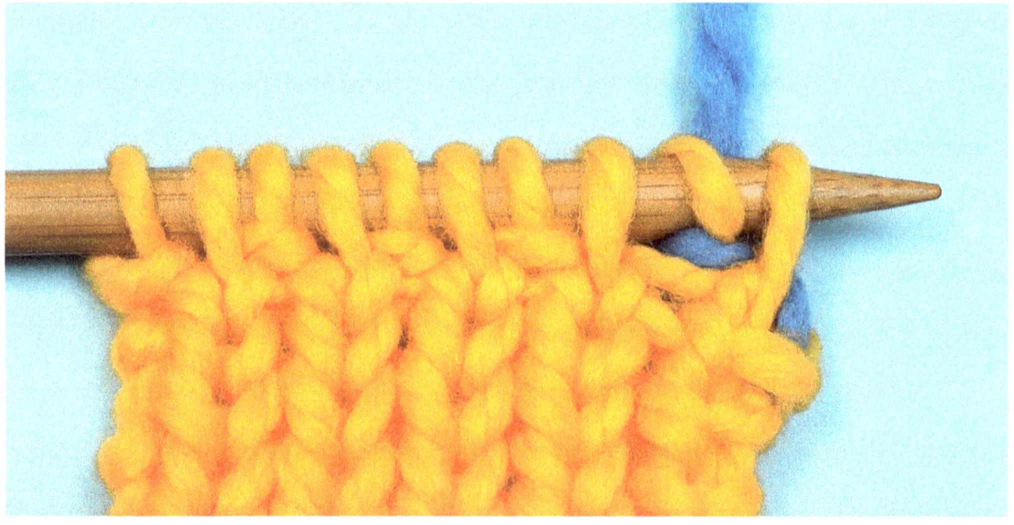

STEP 2

With the right side of the fabric facing you, insert the wool needle from left to right (front to back) **into the first knit stitch** on the left needle.

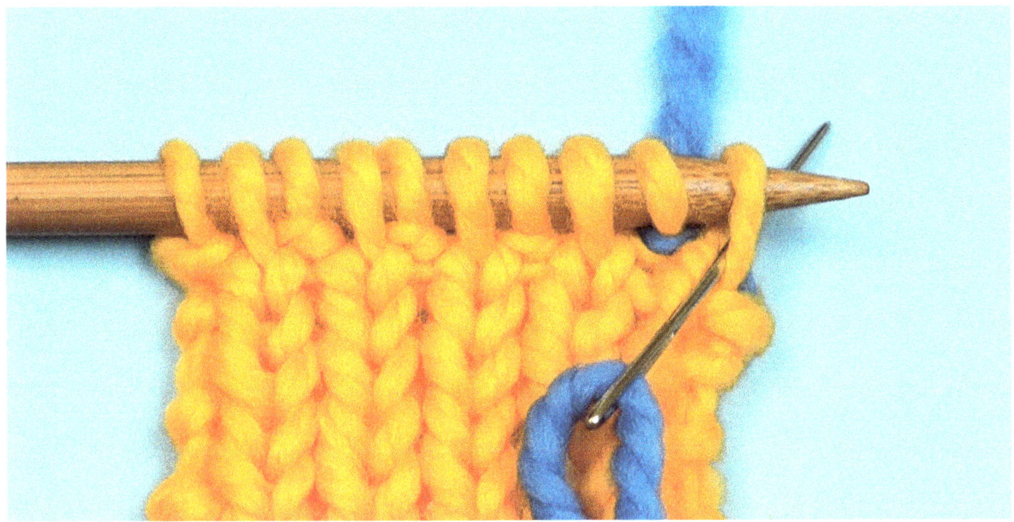

Drop **this knit stitch** off the knitting needle. Then **drop the purl stitch** that we "worked" in the previous step.

Insert the wool needle from right to left (back to front) **into the next knit stitch.**

Drop this knit stitch off the left needle and **pull the yarn** through, but don't pull it too tight. The strand that you form should be as long as **one leg of an average stitch** of the fabric.

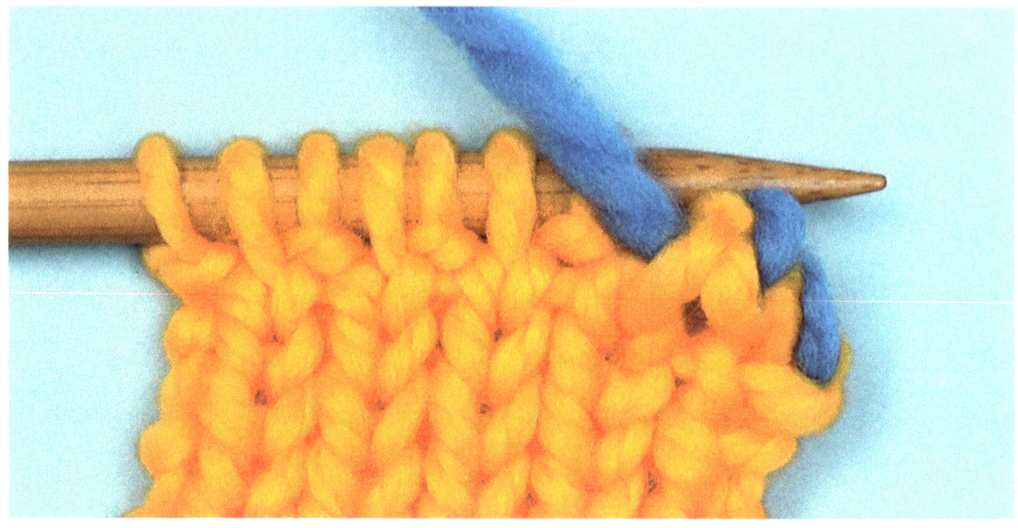

STEP 3

Rotate the fabric **around the left needle** so that you can see the wrong side of the last few rows of the project.

Insert the wool needle **from front to back** into the "previously worked" knit stitch (as it presents itself on this side of the fabric) and **from back to front** into the next knit stitch.

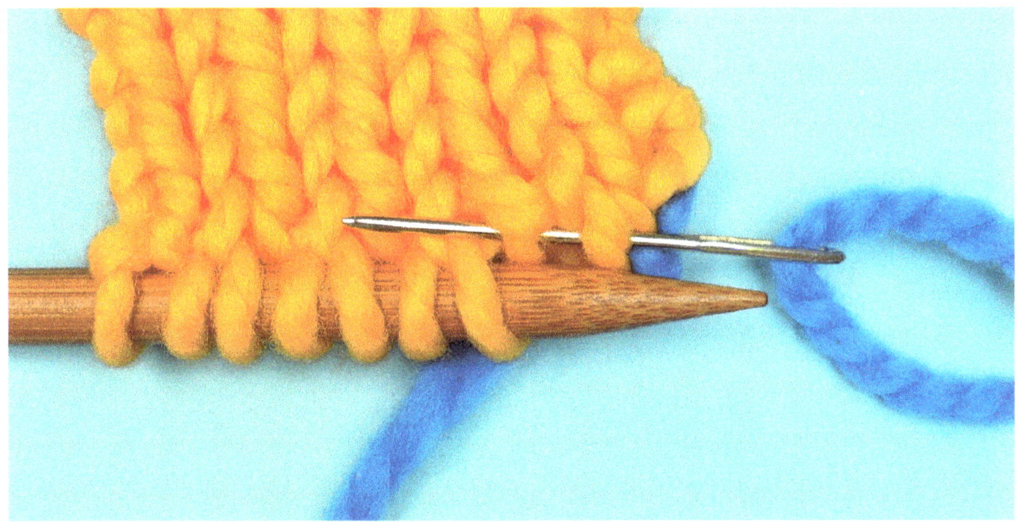

Slip this knit stitch off the knitting needle and pull the yarn through, forming a **neat strand on top** of the edge.

STEP 4

Rotate the work again so that the **right side of the fabric is facing you**, and insert the wool needle from front to back into the "previously worked" knit stitch and from back to front into the next knit stitch.

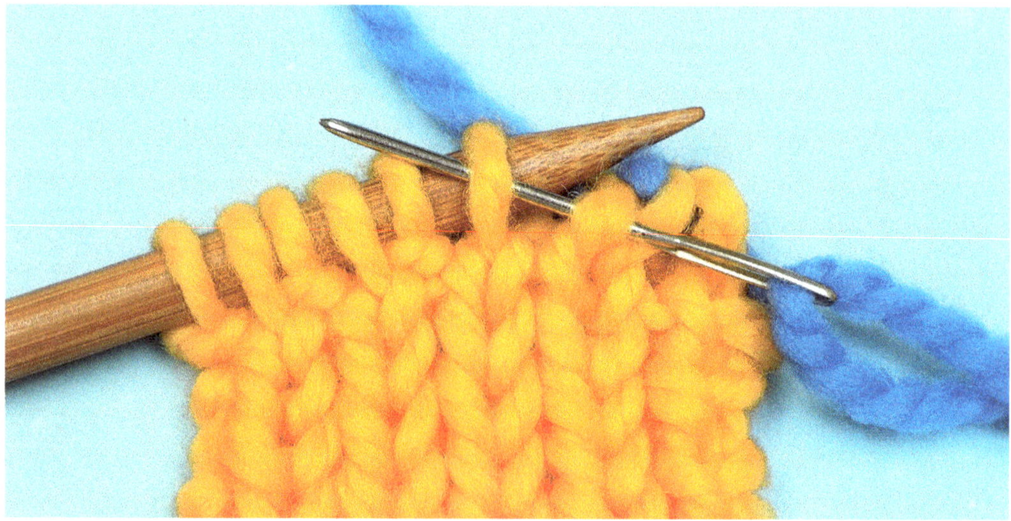

Drop the **knit stitch off the left needle** and pull the yarn through, forming a neat strand on top of the edge.

Repeat **steps 3 and 4** until you bind off all stitches.

It is important to treat the process of **seaming as embroidery**. Because we form each strand separately, we should make sure all strands are of approximately the same length. Otherwise, the bind-off edge will **look a bit sloppy.** Not something we want for our projects, right?

To finish the seam, insert the wool needle **from front to back** into the last knit stitch and **from right to left** into the last purl stitch.

Pull tight, secure the yarn, and hide the tail inside the edge.

TUBULAR BIND OFF FOR 1X1 RIBBING WORKED IN THE ROUND

To add this neat elastic edge to **toe-up socks, neck bands** of bottom-up sweaters, cuffs of top-down sweaters, and **other seamless projects,** we follow a process that is very similar to the one that we used when we worked tubular bind off back and forth, but with **a few tweaks**.

PREPARATION ROUNDS

To give the edge a nice rounded look and to prevent it from flaring out, we'll work **two preparation rounds** before we start to bind off stitches.

You can easily skip these rounds and move to the "Bind Off Itself" section right away, but for best results, take a few extra minutes to work the preparation rounds that will **properly set up the scene** for your beautiful edging.

PREPARATION ROUND 1

Knit 1 stitch, then bring the **yarn to the front** of the work, and slip 1 stitch purlwise to the right needle.

Repeat this sequence **to the end of the round**.

Because in a majority of cases, 1x1 ribbing **starts with a knit stitch**, we'll assume that the first stitch on your left needle is a knit.

If the round in your project **starts with a purl**, slip the first stitch purlwise with the **yarn in front** of the work, and then repeat the sequence described above.

PREPARATION ROUND 2

Because we don't turn the work when we knit in the round, the second preparation round will be **different from the first one**.

Bring the **yarn to the back** of the work and slip 1 stitch purlwise to the right needle, then purl 1 stitch.

Repeat this sequence **to the end of the round**.

If your round **starts with a purl stitch**, purl the first stitch, and then repeat the sequence described above.

These two rounds **form the "tube"** that, as we've already determined on page 119, is valuable to the overall look and feel of this bind-off edge. Now that this tube is in place, we can **move on to the final part** of the process—the bind off itself.

BIND OFF ITSELF

The process of closing the stitches **is the same** as the process we followed when we worked this bind off flat (see pages 130-135).

The only difference is the fact that **we need to seamlessly join** the edge in the round.

To make it easier for us to find the edge stitches, we'll take one proactive step—**attach a locking stitch marker** or a safety pin to the first knit stitch and to the first purl stitch of the round. This helpful trick is **especially important** if you use fine yarn or a yarn in a dark colour.

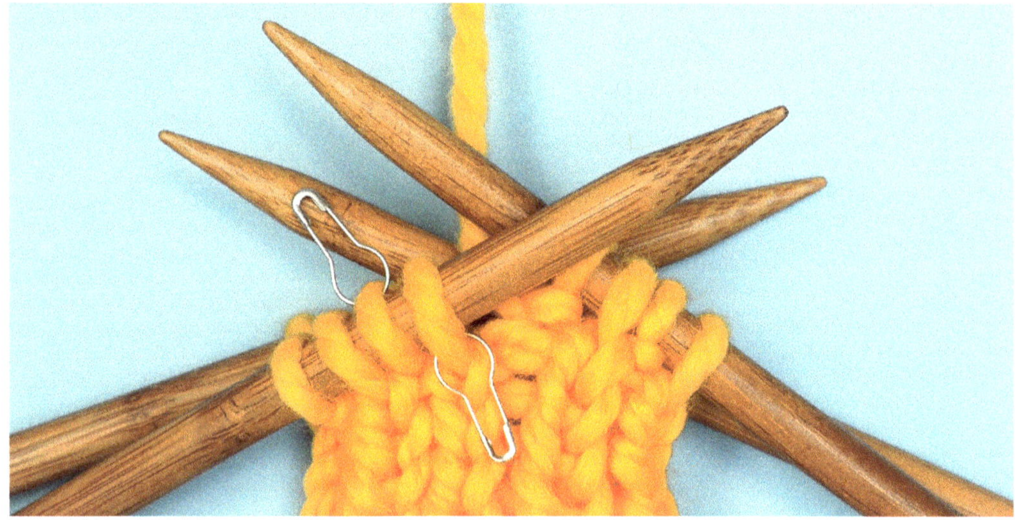

Measure a **pretty long tail** (around three times the length of the bind-off edge), cut the yarn, and thread it into a wool needle.

Follow **steps 1 through 4** described on pages 130-134, and then repeat **steps 3 and 4** until you bind off all stitches and your knitting needles are empty.

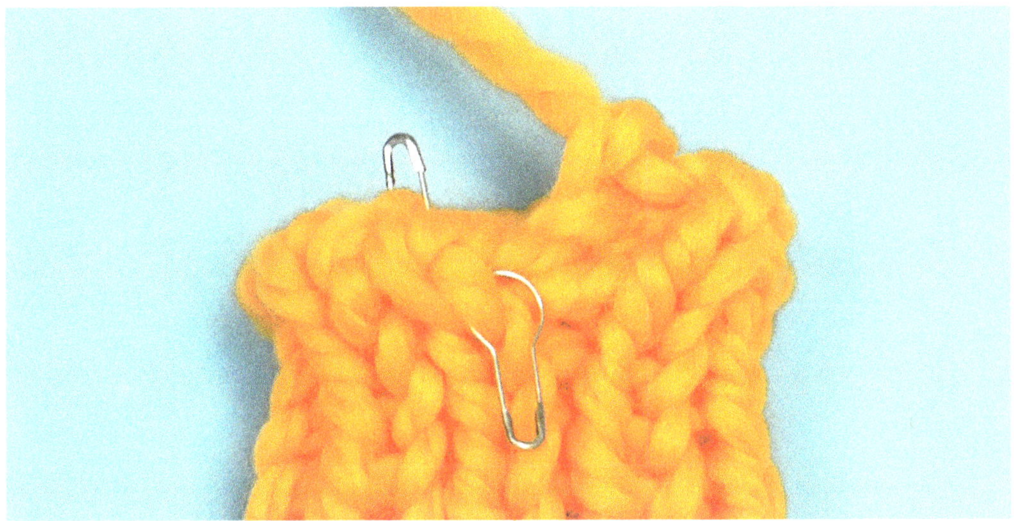

FINISHING THE BIND OFF

This is the time when we'll be glad that we marked the first two stitches of the round. As we **join the last knit and the first knit stitches** of the round on both sides of the fabric, the markers will clearly show us where the first stitches are.

STEP 1

With the **right side of the fabric** facing you, insert the wool needle from front to back into the **last knit stitch** of the round and from back to front into the **first knit stitch** of the round (this is the stitch with a marker attached to it).

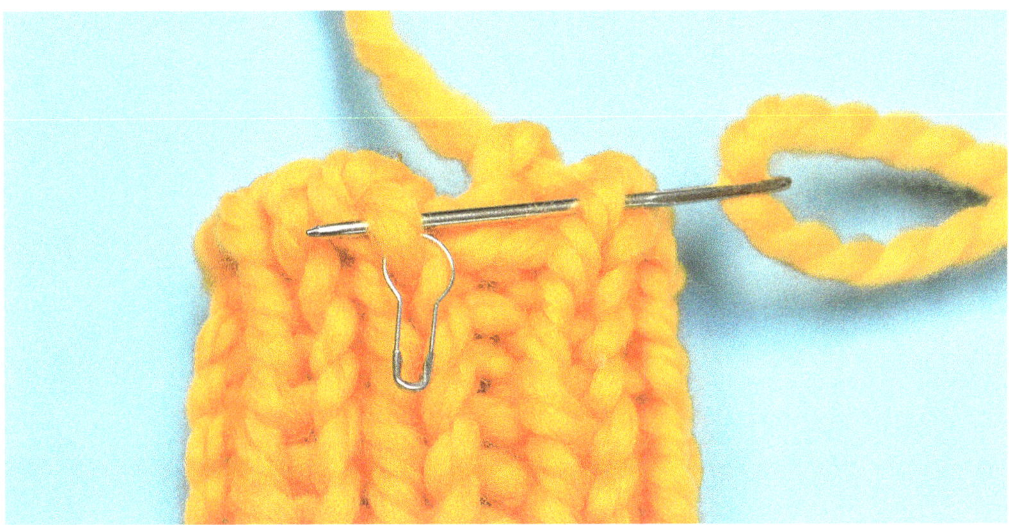

Remove the marker and **pull the yarn through,** forming a neat strand on top of the edge.

STEP 2

Fold the edge so that you could **see the wrong side of the fabric.**

Insert the wool needle from front to back **into the last knit stitch** of the round (as it presents itself on the wrong side of the work), and from back to front **into the first knit stitch** (the one with the marker).

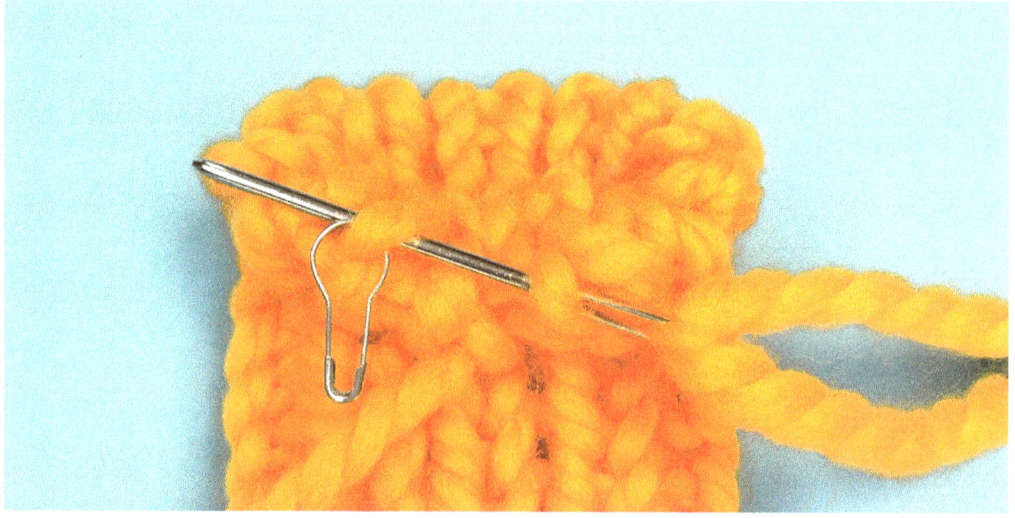

Remove the marker and **pull the yarn through,** forming the last strand on top of the edge.

Secure the yarn and **hide the yarn tail** inside the tubular edge.

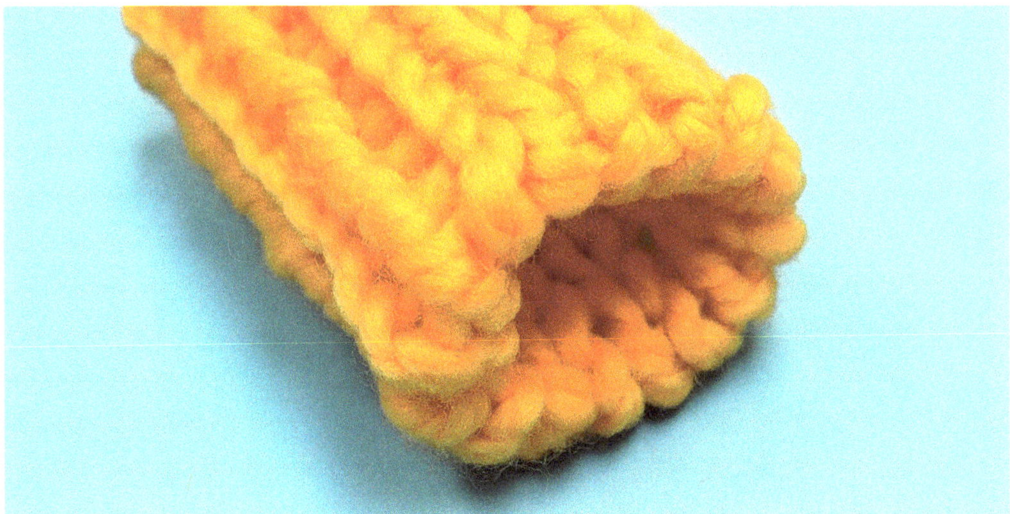

Tubular bind off forms a beautiful edge on a fabric worked in **any stitch pattern**. Even a humble stockinette stitch will get an upgrade with this edging. But, of course, **this method really shines** when we use it to form an elastic edge on projects worked in **"knit 1, purl 1" ribbing**.

TUBULAR CAST ON AND BIND OFF FOR 2X2 RIBBING

As we discovered in the previous chapter, when we use the tubular cast-on method, we cast on stitches in a **sequence of one knit and one purl,** so when we start to work in a "knit 1, purl 1" ribbing pattern, the ribbing **seems to grow out of nowhere,** just like ribbing on manufactured sweaters.

But what if we want to add this edge to projects worked in other types of ribbing? Though it is quite difficult to adjust tubular cast on to a wide ribbing like 3x3, 4x4, or 5x5, there is a **fairly easy way** to make it work for a **"knit 2, purl 2"** rib.

Let's see how we can make it happen.

TUBULAR CAST ON FOR 2X2 RIBBING WORKED FLAT

The cast on itself is **exactly the same** as the cast on we used when we formed tubular cast on for 1x1 ribbing.

STEP 1. CAST ON

Work steps **1 through 4** described on pages. 112-116, then repeat steps **3 and 4** (pages 114-116) until you cast on as many stitches as you need for your project.

Most often, "knit 2, purl 2" ribbing is worked on **multiples of 4 stitches,** with the **first stitch of the row being a knit** stitch. This is the assumption we'll use when we discuss tubular cast on in this chapter.

To make the swatch shown in the photos below, I cast on 12 stitches.

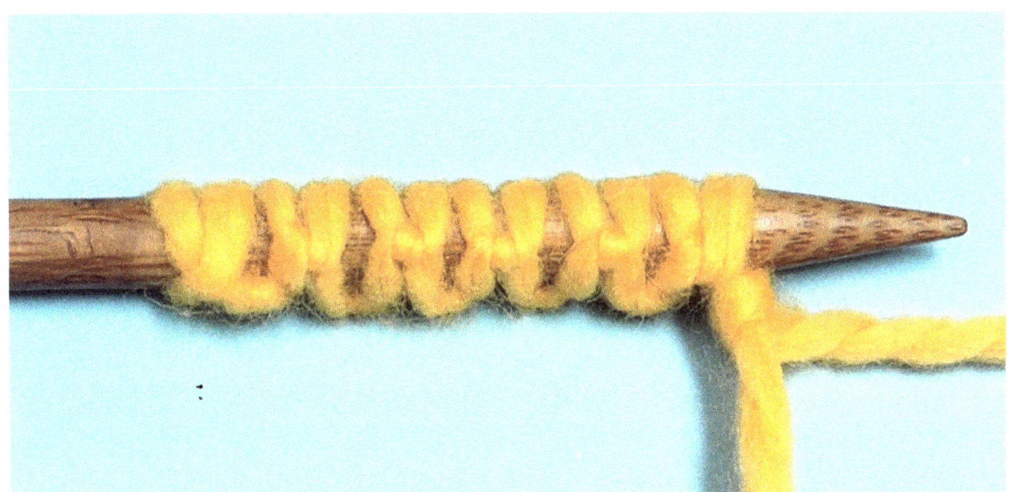

STEP 2. SETUP ROWS

Work **two setup rows** the same way as we did when we added tubular cast on edge to a swatch worked **in 1x1 ribbing**. These rows are described on pages 119-121.

STEP 3. REARANGING STITCHES

Now we are all set for working in the "knit 1, purl 1" ribbing. But that's not exactly what we want, right? We plan to work in the "knit 2, purl 2" ribbing, and that means that we should **rearrange stitches**.

That is exactly what we are going to do in this row.

3.1. Knit the first stitch.

3.2. Insert the tip of the right needle **from left to right** into the next two stitches as if you are going to knit them together.

Ease the left needle out, **slipping these stitches** to the right needle.

3.3. Insert the tip of the left needle **from left to right** into the slipped stitches, then take the right needle out, **returning these stitches** to the left needle.

3.4. Knit one stitch **through the back loop**.

3.5. Bring the **yarn to the front** of the work, and insert the right needle from left to right **under the back leg** of the first stitch of the left needle.

Wrap the tip of the right needle with the yarn **as we do when we purl** a stitch, and pull this wrap through, purling this stitch **through the back loop**.

3.6. Purl the next stitch as usual, **through the front loop**.

Repeat **steps 3.1 through 3.6** to the end of the row.

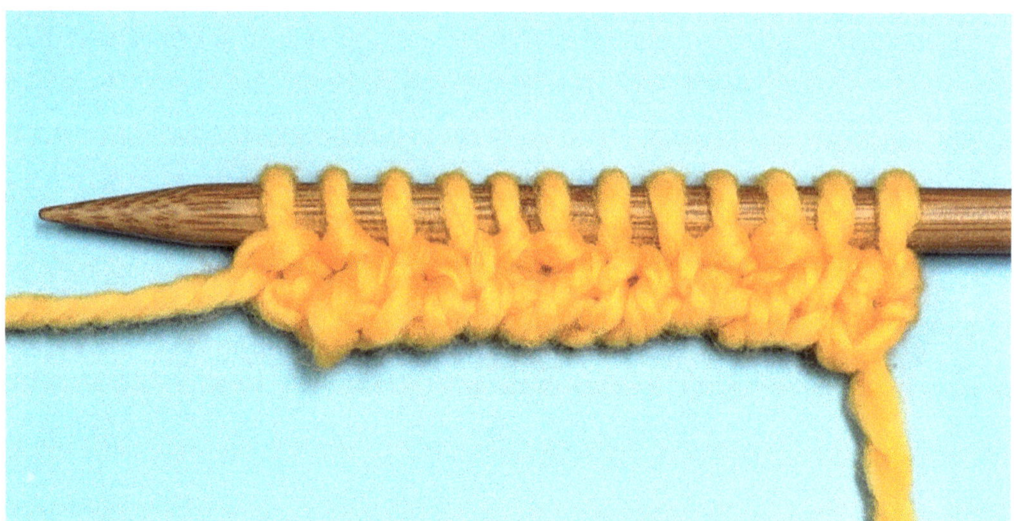

As you see, all **stitches are now lined up** for working in the "knit 2, purl 2" ribbing pattern, and we can make this ribbing knowing that the cast-on edge that we formed is elastic, fully reversible, and consistent with the structure of 2x2 ribbing.

TUBULAR CAST ON FOR 2X2 RIBBING WORKED IN THE ROUND

To add this cast on edge to a seamless project, **we are going to cheat.** Instead of fiddling with yarn wraps, we'll join stitches for working in the round **only after we work the setup rows**.

It is the **easiest and least confusing way** to apply this cast-on method to a project worked in the round, and there is no reason not to make our life easier.

STEP 1. CAST ON

We start by casting on a **multiple of 4 stitches using steps 1-4** described on pages 112-116. Then we **repeat steps 3 and 4** (pages 114-116) until we cast on all stitches that we need for our seamless project.

My swatch will be worked on **16 stitches**, so this is the number of stitches that I cast on.

STEP 2. SETUP ROWS

Turn the work and follow the **instructions on pages 119-121** to make two setup rows. That's right—we are not working in the round just yet.

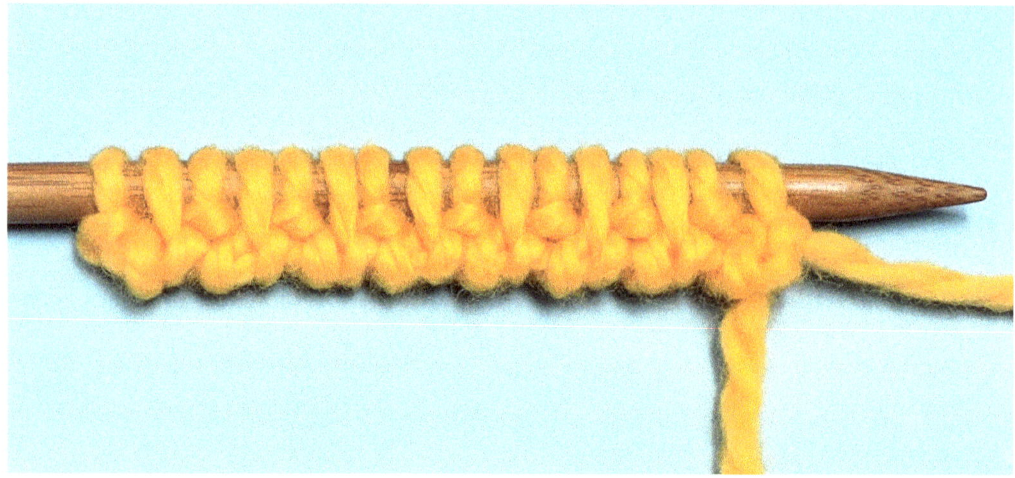

STEP 3. SETUP ROUND

This is the time when we **start to work in the round** while, at the same time, regrouping stitches into the "knit 2, purl 2" sequence.

First, **arrange the stitches for working in the round** using any setup that you like. I will use five double-pointed needles, so I divided all stitches into four equal groups and moved each group to a separate needle.

Place the work on a flat surface, and make sure all sections of the edge are **inside the circle** formed by the needles.

Don't join stitches in any special way. To eliminate the possible gap between the first and the last stitches of the round, **pull the yarn slightly** after you knit the first stitch.

If you work with one short circular needle, **place a marker** to mark the beginning of the round. For other methods, it is perfectly fine to **use the yarn tail** as a way to remind you where the round begins.

Now that we are all set for working in the round, repeat **steps 3.1 through 3.6** (pages 144-148) to the end of the round.

Work in 2x2 ribbing for as long as it is required for your project.

STEP 4. FIXING THE GAP

As you work a few rounds, you will see that the **setup rows created a small gap** between the first and the last cast-on stitches.

This gap is **easy to fix**. We can do it after we work a few rounds, or when we weave in the yarn tails.

Simply thread the yarn tail into a wool needle and **work steps 4.1 and 4.2 described on pages 125-126.** Then secure the yarn and hide the tail inside the edge.

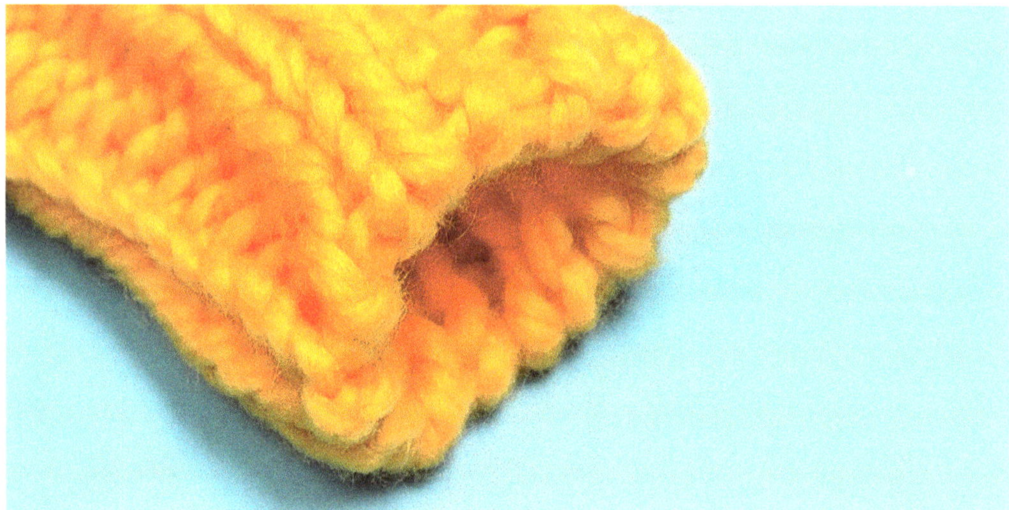

Just as they did for the tubular cast on for 1x1 ribbing, these steps make sure the **join is perfectly invisible** when we add this cast on edge to a seamless project worked in 2x2 ribbing.

TUBULAR BIND OFF FOR 2X2 RIBBING WORKED FLAT

Now that we know how **neat and elastic tubular edge** is, naturally, we want to form it when we bind off stitches of a project worked in 2x2 ribbing,

Just as we did when we bound off stitches worked in "knit 1, purl 1" ribbing, we'll use a wool needle, and **we'll close stitches in pairs**. To keep things simple, we'll rotate the fabric around the knitting needle so that we can deal only with knit stitches. We'll also remember to **work each stitch twice**.

Even though preparation rows do keep the edge from flaring out, in 2x2 ribbing they interfere too much with the elasticity of the fabric. That's why we are going to **skip these rows** and start to bind off stitches right away.

Here's how we do it **step by step**.

STEP 1. SETUP

Cut the yarn, leaving a tail that is **at least three times as long** as the bind-off edge. Thread this long tail into a wool needle.

To make it easier for you to see how each step is worked, I attached a piece of yarn in a contrasting colour as the yarn tail in my swatch.

In most cases, 2x2 **ribbing starts with two knit stitches**, and that's the assumption we'll use as we discuss this bind-off method in this chapter.

To make sure the right-hand side of the fabric looks neat, we need to **make an extra step** before we get to the main part of binding off stitches. This preparation step is **required only** when we bind off stitches of a **fabric worked back and forth**.

STEP 2. PREPARATION

With the **right side of the work facing you**, insert the wool needle from front to back (left to right) into the first knit stitch from the tip of the knitting needle.

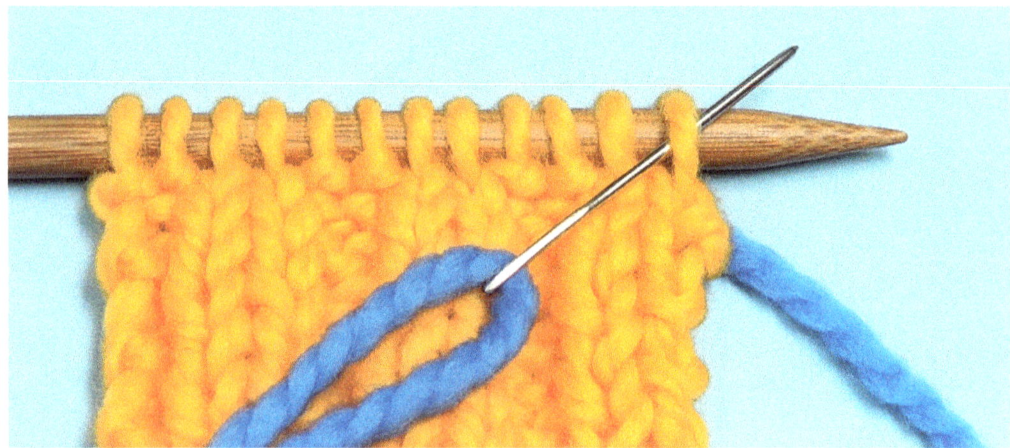

Slip this stitch off the knitting needle, then **rotate the fabric** so that you can see the wrong side of the work, and insert the wool needle **from back to front** into the **first knit stitch on the wrong side** of the fabric (it will be the third stitch of the row).

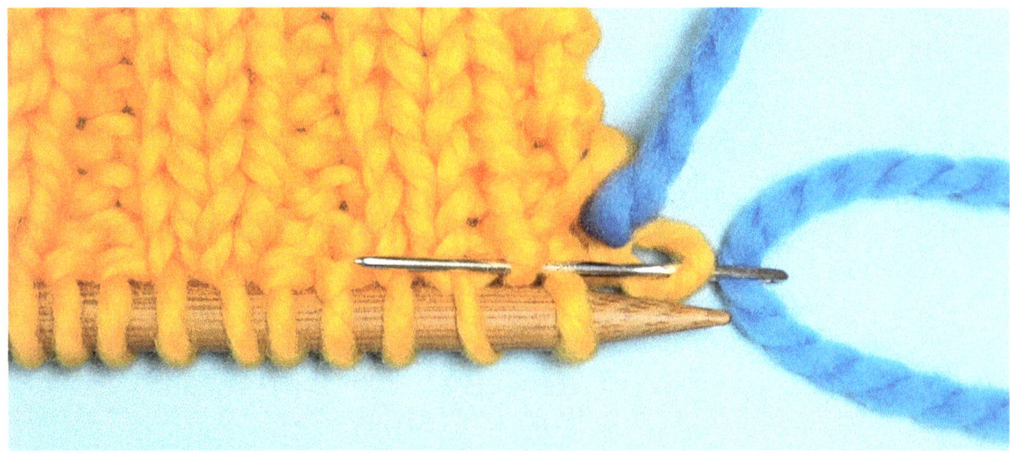

Pull the yarn through, but **don't pull it too tight**. To make sure the edge is fully invisible, each strand on top of the edge should be approximately **as long as one leg** of an average stitch in this row.

STEP 3

With the **right side of the work facing you**, insert the wool needle **from front to back** into the "previously worked" knit stitch and **from back to front** (right to left) into the next knit stitch.

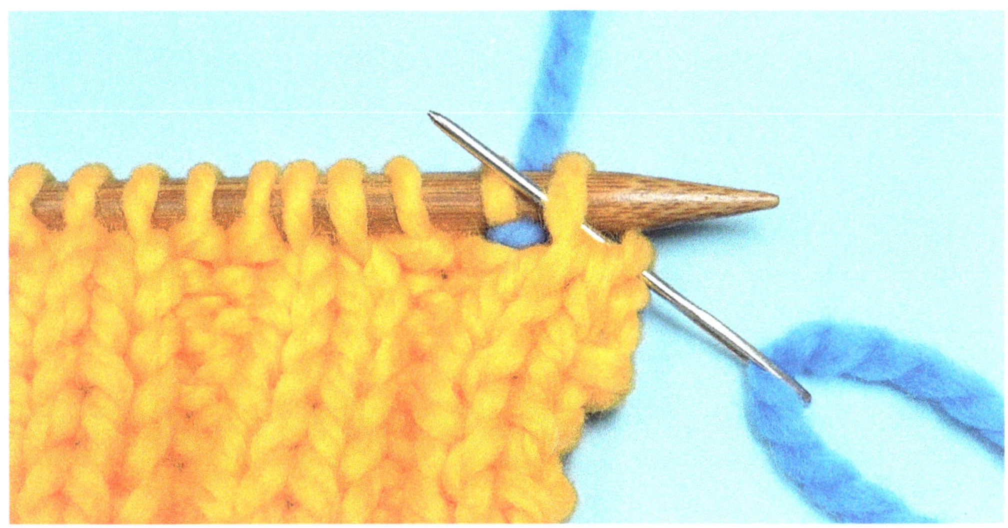

Slip this knit stitch off the knitting needle, pull the yarn through, and **adjust the length of the strand** on top of the edge.

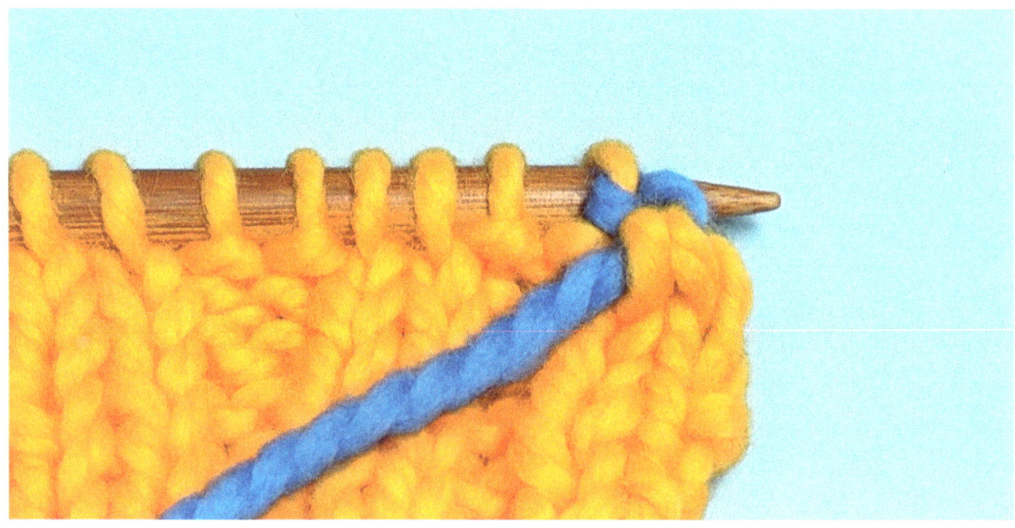

STEP 4

Move the fabric around the knitting needle so that you could **see the wrong side** of the work, and insert the wool needle from front to back (right to left) into the **"previously worked" knit stitch.**

Slip this stitch off the knitting needle and insert the wool needle from back to front into the **next knit stitch**.

Slip this knit stitch off the knitting needle, pull the yarn through, and **form a neat strand on top** of the edge.

STEP 5

This step is **similar to step 3**, but this time, we'll join the last knit stitch in the previous column with the first knit stitch in the next column of stitches.

With the **right side of the work facing you**, insert the wool needle from front to back into the **"previously worked" knit stitch** and from back to front into the **next knit stitch** (the first stitch on the knitting needle).

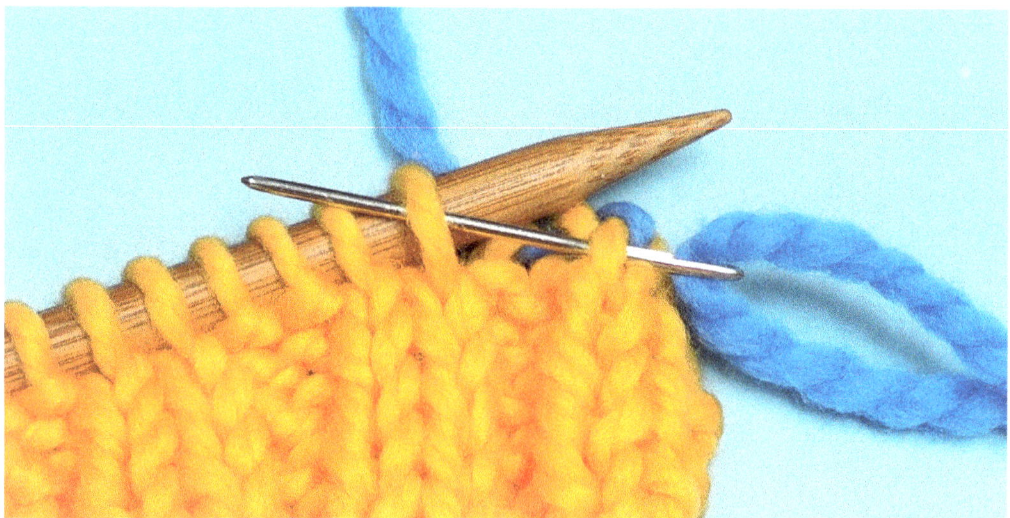

Slip this knit stitch off the knitting needle and pull the yarn through, forming a **neat strand on top** of the edge.

STEP 6

Now let's **join two columns of knit stitches** on the wrong side of the work.

Rotate the fabric to see the stitches **on the wrong side**, and insert the wool needle **from front to back** into the last knit stitch in the previous column of knit stitches.

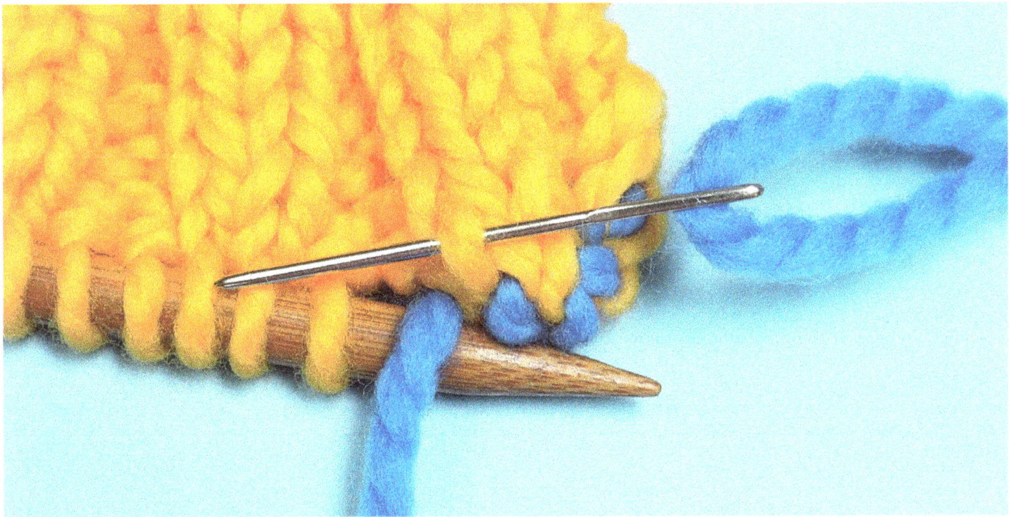

Then insert the wool needle **from back to front** into the next knit stitch. Because this stitch is the second one from the tip of the knitting needle, we need to **go around the first stitch**. It is a bit inconvenient, but not difficult.

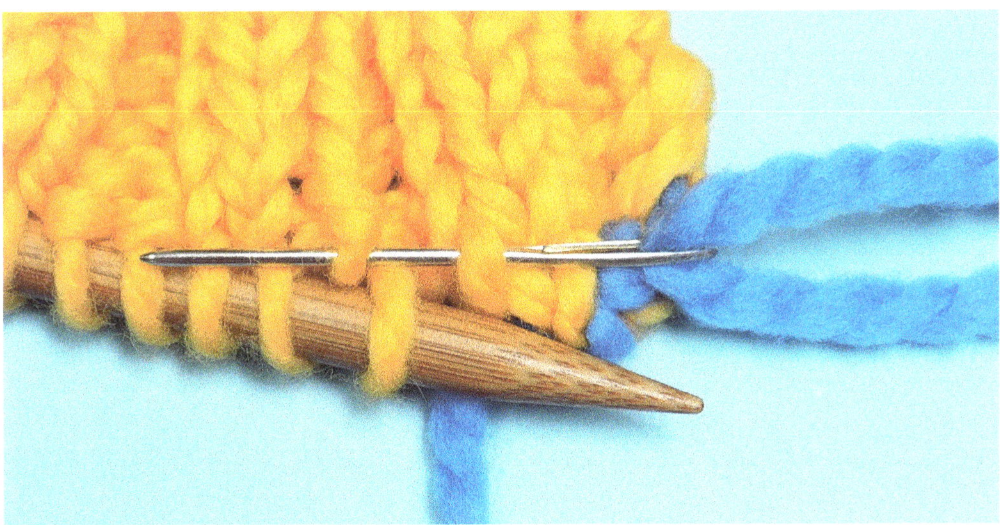

The first stitch on the knitting needle is **not secured**, and we can't slip it off the needle just yet. That's why, in this step, we pull the yarn through **without slipping any stitches** off the knitting needle.

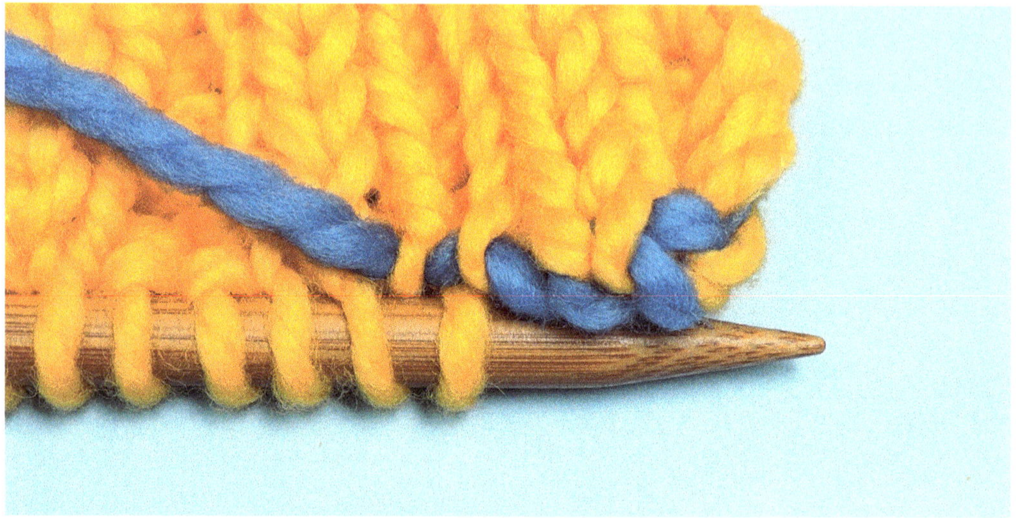

We'll slip both these stitches right after we work steps 3 and 4 again.

Repeat **steps 3 through 6** until you bind off all stitches. If the ribbing in your project ends with two purls, you will finish binding off stitches **after you work step 4**.

FINISHING THE BIND OFF

To make sure the left-hand side of the project is as nice-looking as its right-hand side, insert the wool needle **from front to back** into the last knit stitch **on the right side** of the work, and from front to back into the last stitch of the row.

Pull the yarn through and **form the last strand on top** of the edge. Secure the yarn and hide the yarn tail on the wrong side of the work, or inside the edge if the project is reversible.

This edge is **neat, stretchy, and fully reversible**. It does not look like a stiff bind-off edge we get when we use other methods, and it is consistent with the structure of the "knit 2, purl 2" ribbing.

TUBULAR BIND OFF FOR 2X2 RIBBING WORKED IN THE ROUND

To add this edge to a seamless project, we follow a **process that is very similar** to the one that we used when we added tubular bind off to a project worked flat.

The only challenge we face is the need to make the edge fully seamless by **joining the first and last knit stitches** on both sides of the fabric.

To make it easier for us to find the first stitches when it is time to join them to the last stitches of the round, we **attach a locking stitch marker** or a safety pin to the first knit stitch on the right side of the fabric and the first knit stitch on the wrong side of the work.

Now we are **ready to bind off** stitches.

Work **steps 3 and 4** described on pages 155-157.

Because we don't work step 2 when we bind off stitches of a seamless project, we insert the wool needle **into the first stitches of the round** instead of the "previously worked" stitches.

Then work **steps 5 and 6** described on pages 158-160.

Repeat **steps 3 through 6** until you have no more stitches on the knitting needles.

Then work **two simple steps** described below. These steps will make sure the bind-off edge is as seamless as the project itself.

STEP 1

With the **right side of the fabric facing you**, insert the wool needle from front to back into the **last knit stitch** of the round and from back to front into the **first knit stitch** of the round. This is the stitch marked with a stitch marker.

Remove the marker and **pull the yarn through,** forming a neat strand on top of the edge.

STEP 2

Fold the fabric so that you can see **the wrong side of the work** and insert the wool needle from front to back into the **last knit stitch** and from back to front into the **first knit stitch** of the round.

Remove the marker and **pull the yarn through,** forming the last strand on top of the bind-off edge.

Secure the yarn and weave in the yarn tail.

Tubular bind off has a **pleasant rhythm**, and even though there are a number of steps involved, the **process quickly becomes satisfying**, like a process of putting together a simple puzzle.

JUDY'S MAGIC CAST ON AND GRAFTING

STRETCH ★★★★★

DIFFICULTY ★★★☆☆

TOOLS

The last pair of methods that we are going to discuss in this book creates the **most invisible edges**.

In fact, they are not even edges in the true sense of the word. They look like a **piece of stockinette fabric folding** to form a double-layered project.

These edges are perfect for hems, seamless totes, toys, and all sorts of bands, and they are **indispensable for making socks**. Judy's magic cast on is a great way to start toe-up socks, and grafting is the best way to finish top-down ones.

Because these methods form a seamless double-layered fabric, it is hard to say whether they are worked flat or in the round. So we'll consider them to be unique, and **we won't label them** as "worked flat" or "worked in the round".

JUDY'S MAGIC CAST ON

There are **many modifications** to the original Magic Cast On that was *developed by Judy Becker* almost 20 years ago. I tested all the variations that I could find and came up with a **way that is the easiest** and the most efficient.

The method explained in this chapter is a blend of several adjustments, and it **works well for different setups** that allow us to knit in the round. You can use this method when you work with double-pointed needles, two circular needles, or one long circular needle used with the **magic loop method**.

It could be a bit tricky to make this cast on with a very short circular needle, so I wouldn't recommend it.

SETUP STEP 1

Align two needles and **hold them in your right hand** so that one needle is at the top and the other one is at the bottom.

SETUP STEP 2

Take the yarn in your left hand and place the strand between the needles from **back to front.**

Then move the tail **over the top needle**, making a yarn wrap. This wrap forms **the first stitch** on the top needle.

This part is different from the original method described by Judy Becker. We **start with a yarn wrap** and not with a slip knot.

Slip knot is not flexible, and it often **causes visible stiffness** at one side of the edge. We can easily avoid it by making a yarn wrap instead.

SETUP STEP 3

Just as we do when we use the **long-tail cast-on** method, place the yarn tail on your left thumb, the working yarn on your left index finger, and hold both strands with your other three left fingers.

If you plan to cast on many stitches, **make sure the yarn tail is long**. To be on the safe side, leave a tail that is **around four times as long** as the future cast-on edge.

This cast on is easy because there are **only three rules** that we need to follow. Here they are:

1. We usually **cast on stitches in pairs**—one stitch on the top needle and one stitch on the bottom needle.

2. We always wrap the yarn around each needle **from the bottom of the needle, to the front, and over the top**. This rule does not only make it easier to remember the process, but it also forms stitches in the **correct orientation** so that we can knit all stitches through the front loop in the first round.

3. We always use the yarn that comes from the thumb (the bottom strand) to add stitches to the top needle and the yarn that comes from the index finger (the top strand) to add stitches to the bottom needle. To make it easy to remember, think **"bottom needle—top strand, top needle—bottom strand"**.

Let's see how these rules work in **two simple steps**.

STEP 1. ADDING A STITCH TO THE BOTTOM NEEDLE

Move the needles so that the **bottom needle lies on the top strand** (the one that comes from your left index finger).

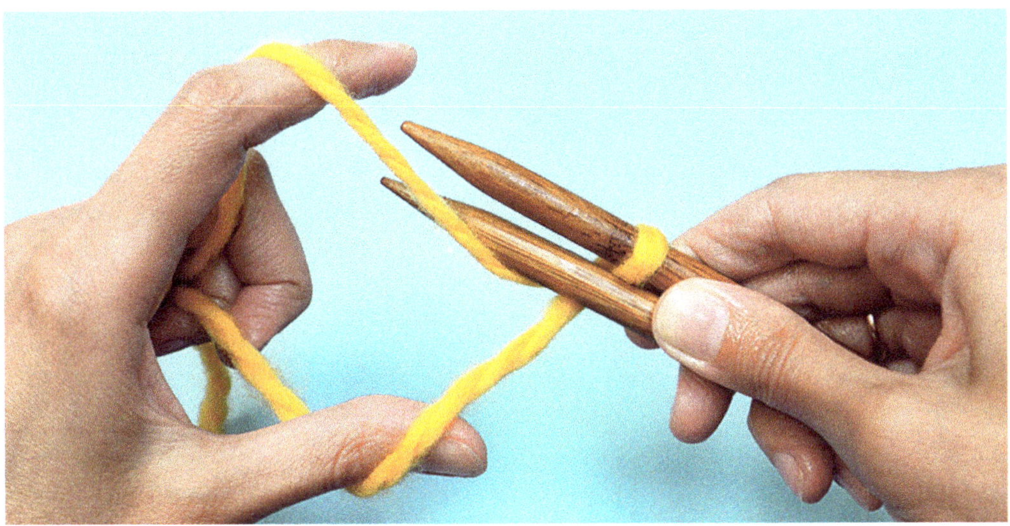

Wrap the top strand **around the bottom needle** from front to back.

The yarn wrap that we've just formed is our next stitch.

STEP 2. ADDING A STITCH TO THE TOP NEEDLE

Move the needles so that the bottom strand (the one that comes from your left thumb) is at the bottom of the top needle. That means that this strand will be **between the needles**.

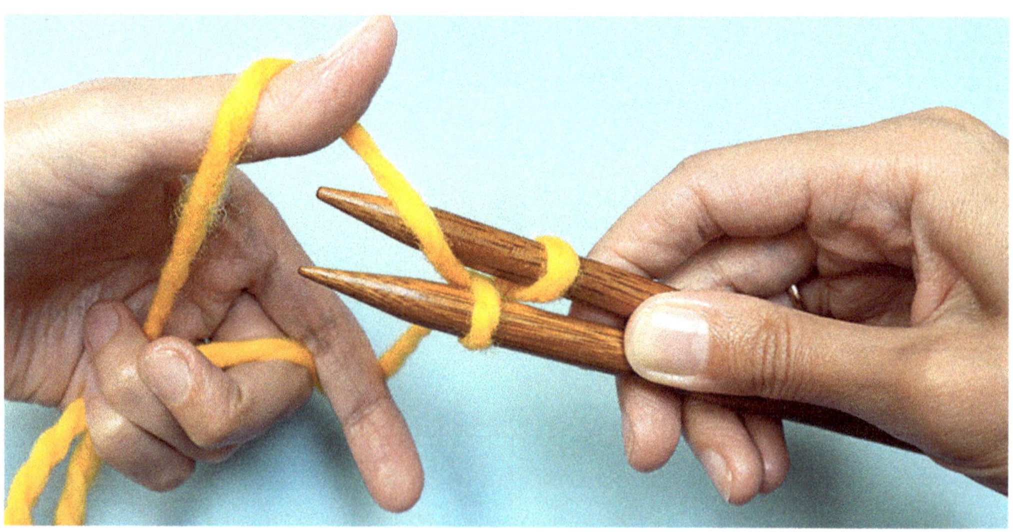

Wrap the bottom strand **around the top needle** from front to back.

We've just formed **another stitch** on the top needle.

Repeat steps 1 and 2 until you make as many stitches as you need for your project.

For example, if the pattern tells you to cast on 20 stitches in total, stop adding stitches when you have 10 stitches on the top needle and 10 stitches on the bottom needle.

Twist the yarn tail and the working yarn after you cast on the last stitch to keep that stitch from unravelling.

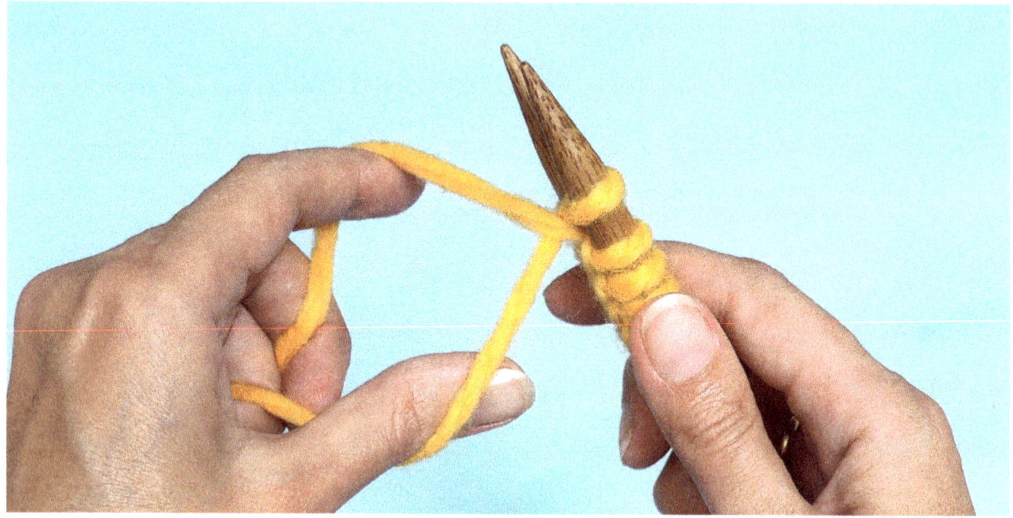

Take both needles in your left hand and **work the first round**.

If you work with two circular needles or one long circular needle and the magic loop method, **pull the bottom needle to the right** to move the bottom set of stitches to the cable of a circular needle. Use the bottom needle to knit the stitches on the top needle.

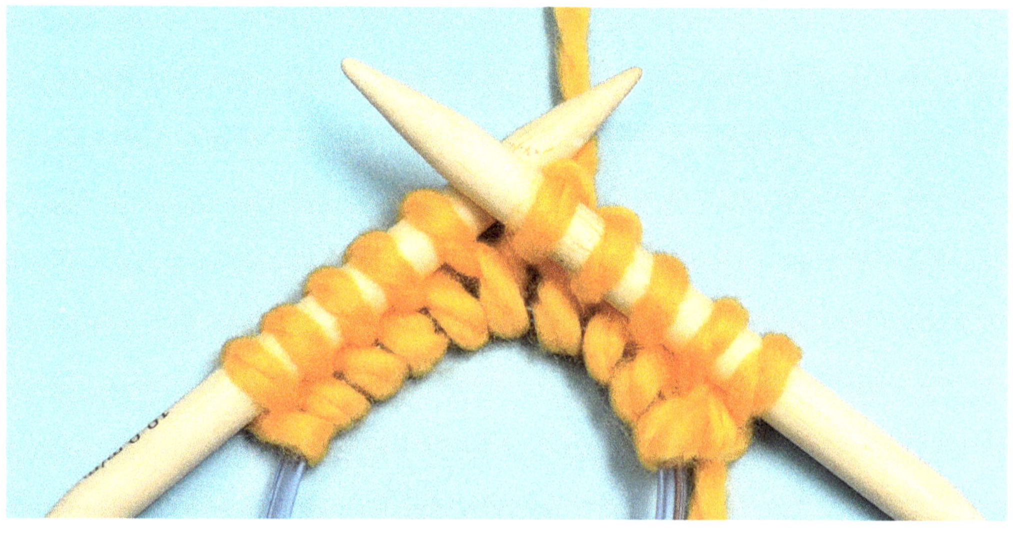

If you work with **double-pointed needles**, knit half of the stitches of each set with one needle and the other half with another needle. This way, you will have all stitches **evenly distributed** between four needles after you finish the first round.

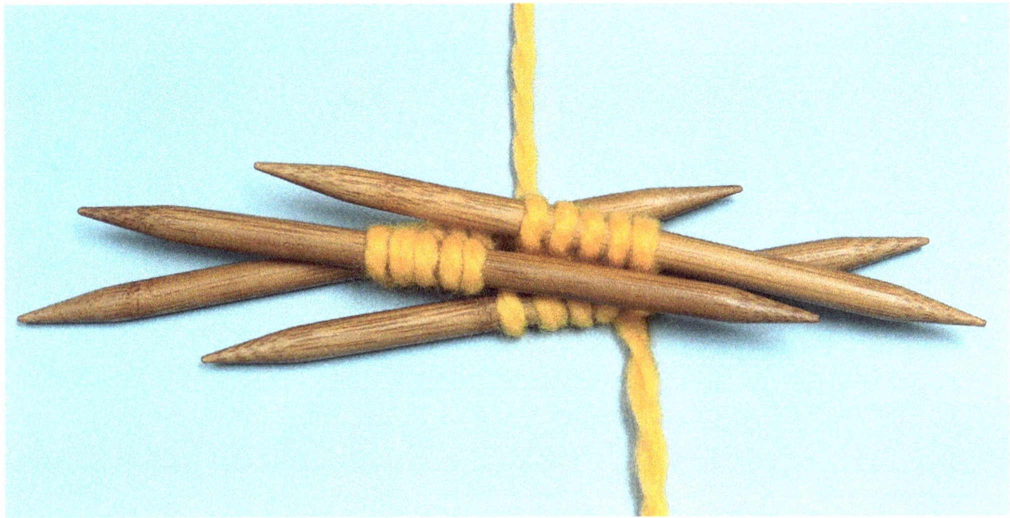

Unlike several other popular seamless cast-on methods, magic cast on **does not form loose stitches at the cast-on edge** even when our tension is not perfect. They don't call it "magic" for no reason.

GRAFTING

This way of closing stitches **differs depending on the stitch pattern** of the pieces that we join using this method.

Because our **goal is to match the look** of the edge formed by the Judy's magic cast-on method (page 168), we'll focus on a variation that allows us to invisibly join **two groups of knit stitches**. This particular variation is also known as the Kitchener stitch.

Many knitters find this super useful method confusing and time-consuming. While it does take time to make this special seam, it is **not difficult at all**. In fact, it can be done in **only two simple steps**.

This method works **the same way** when we join two separate pieces of fabric and when we join two sides of a circular piece that grows from an edge formed by the Judy's magic cast-on method.

As Judy's magic cast on gives a start to a tube, we'll see how we can seamlessly join two groups of stitches of a **circular piece of fabric**.

SETUP

When you are ready to close the stitches, rearrange them so that one half of the stitches is on a knitting **needle at the front** and the other half is on a knitting **needle at the back** of the project.

Just as we did when we used the tubular bind-off method (pages 127 and 153), we'll close stitches with a wool needle. It means that we need to **leave a pretty long yarn tail**. The tail should be around three times as long as the width of the fabric.

Place the project on a flat surface so that the knitting needles are aligned, and both the tips of the needles and the yarn tail are **at the right-hand side** of the project.

To make it easier for you to see how every step of this bind-off method works, I'll use a piece of **yarn in a contrasting colour** as my yarn tail.

Insert the wool needle **from back to front** (right to left) into the first stitch on the knitting needle at the front.

Slip this stitch off the knitting needle and **pull the yarn** all the way through.

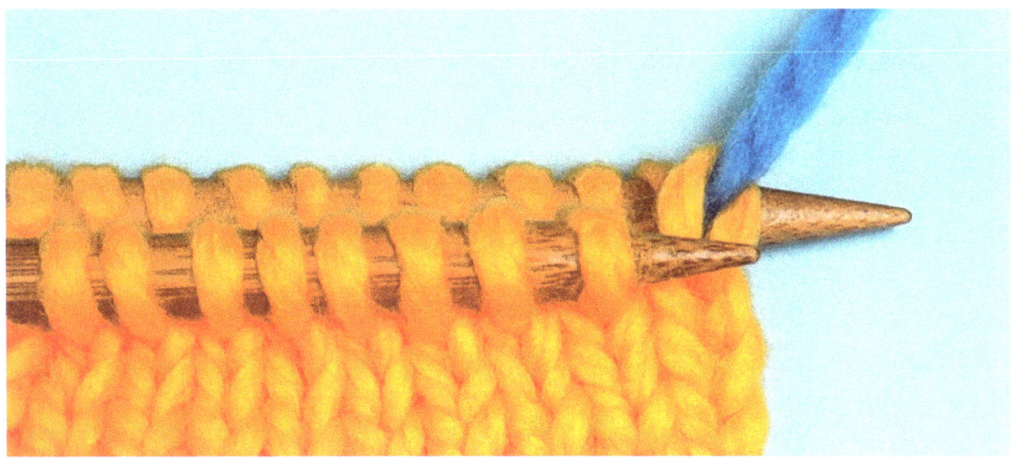

Then insert the wool needle **from left to right** into the first stitch on the knitting needle at the back.

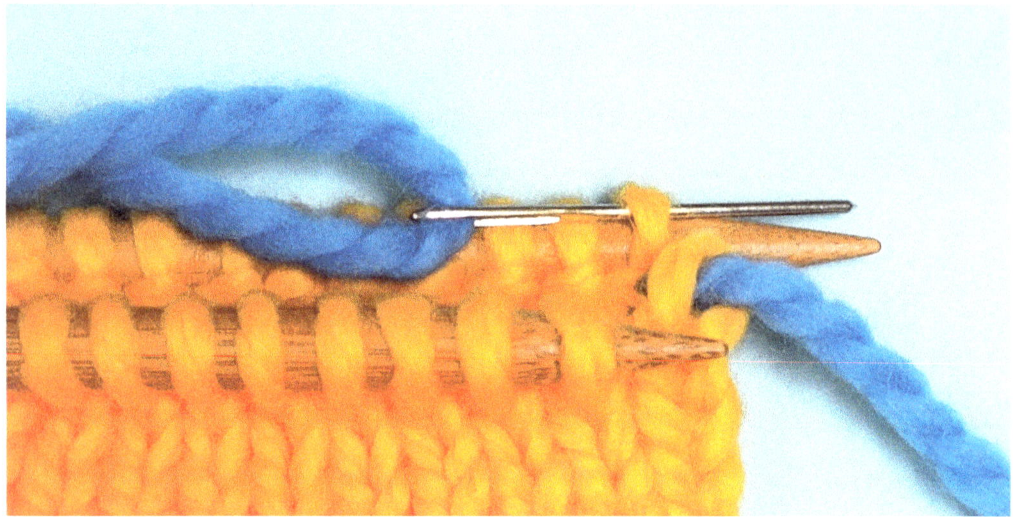

Slip this stitch off the knitting needle and pull the yarn through. This time, **pull it just enough** to form a strand that is **as long as one leg** of an average stitch in the last round of the fabric.

Because we form each strand separately, it is important to treat the process of binding off stitches **a bit like embroidery**. If we carefully craft each strand, the bind off will be completely invisible.

Now we are ready to join these two sets of stitches with an edge that looks **more like a fold** than a line of bound-off stitches.

STEP 1

With the fabric on the **front needle facing you**, insert the wool needle from front to back into the stitch that we've just worked on this side of the fabric. This is our **"previously worked" stitch**.

Then insert the wool needle from back to front **into the next stitch**. It will be the first stitch from the tip of the knitting needle at the front.

Slip this stitch off the knitting needle, **pull the yarn through**, and adjust the size of the strand at the top of the edge.

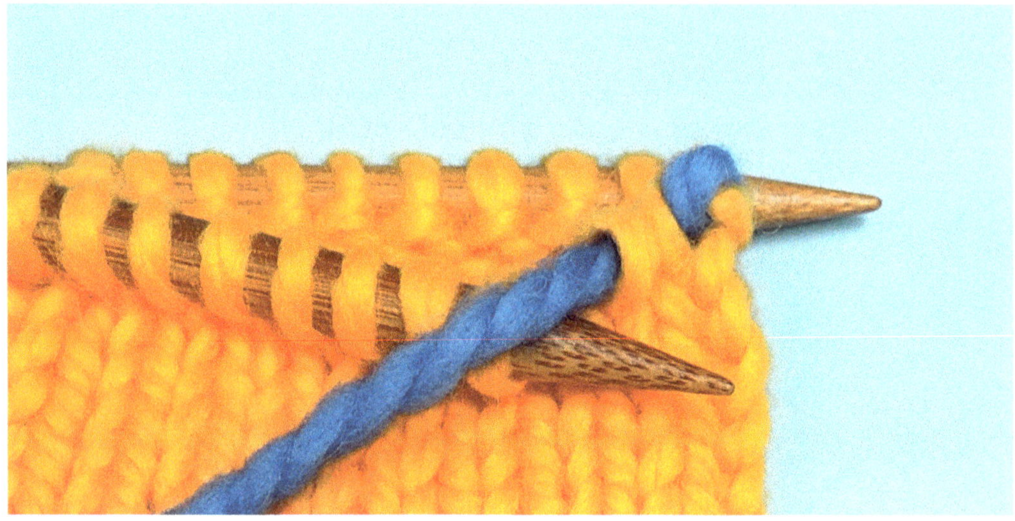

STEP 2

Rotate the work around the knitting needles so that you can see the right side of the stitches that sit on the **knitting needle at the back.**

Insert the wool needle from front to back into the "previously worked" stitch on this side of the fabric.

Then insert the wool needle **from back to front** into the next stitch.

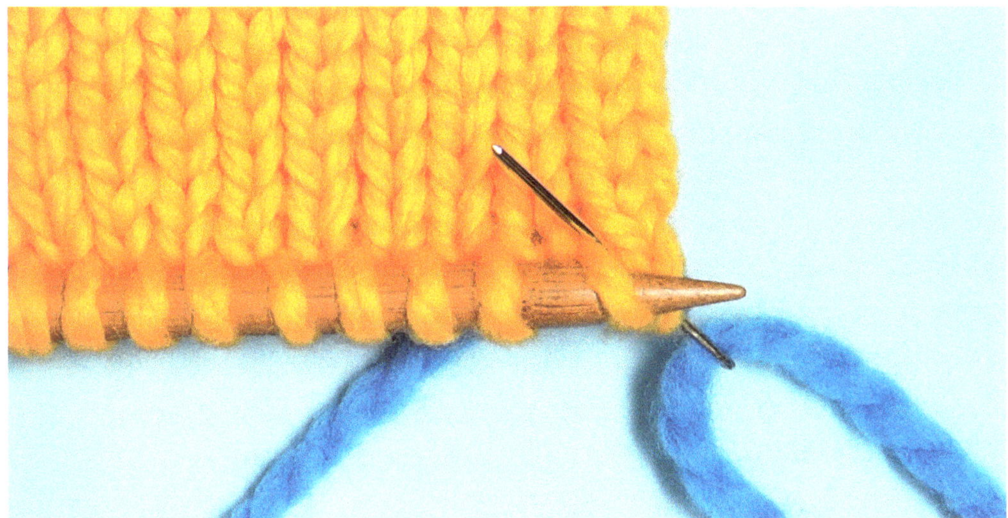

Slip this stitch off the knitting needle and **pull the yarn through,** forming another strand on top of the edge.

Repeat these two steps until you bind off all stitches.

As you pull the yarn through after each step, **hold the bottom of the open stitches** with your left thumb and index fingers. This way, we don't let the pulling distort the fabric, and we **make it easy to find** the "previously worked" stitch when it is time to work it in the next step.

To finish the left-hand side of the bind-off edge, insert the wool needle from front to back into the last stitch at the front of the work and from back to front into the last stitch at the back of the work.

Pull the yarn through and **form the last strand** on top of the bind-off edge.

Secure the yarn and **hide the yarn tail** inside the edge, or snake it through the back of the stitches along the left vertical side of the knitted piece.

HOW TO PREVENT "EARS"

When we use this pair of methods to form horizontal edges on double-layered scarves, blankets, seamless totes, and other **projects that benefit from distinct right angles** at the corners of the fabric, it is safe to use Judy's magic cast on and grafting exactly as they are described in this chapter.

But when we apply these methods to socks, toys, and projects that require **more rounded corners**, the right-angle corners formed by this duo become quite a nuisance.

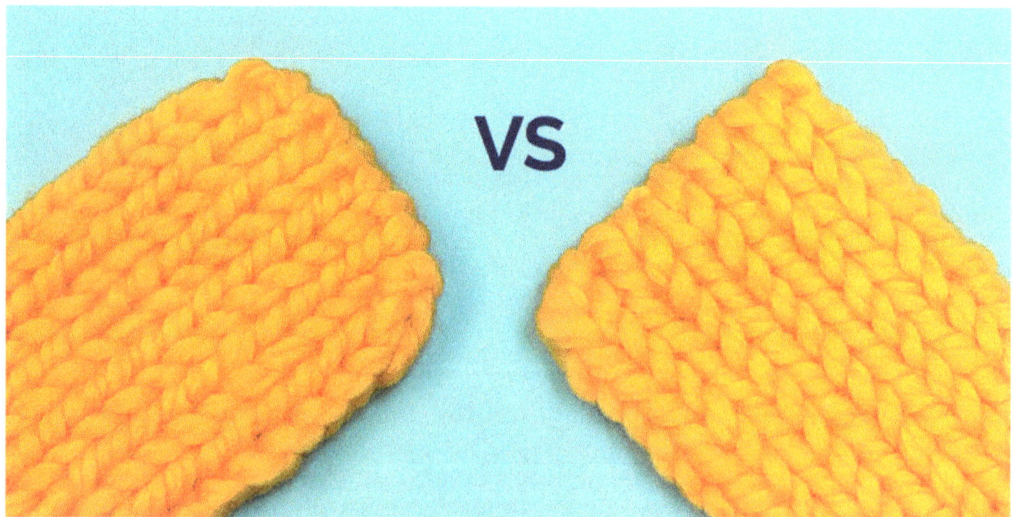

They look a bit like ears, and even though they do not affect the fit, the **project will look more sleek** and well-finished without those pointy stitches.

The "ears" are not formed when we cast on or bind off stitches. They are **formed by the stitches of the last round** of the fabric, and we can minimise the size of the "ears" if we pull the yarn at the very beginning and at the very end of the cast-on or bind-off edge, but this **does not eliminate** the "pointy stitches" completely.

Fortunately, there is a **simple way to get rid** of this issue. Let's see how it works step by step.

In many cases, the **"ears" at the cast on** edge are **not very prominent**, but if you'd like to eliminate them completely, follow these steps:

STEP 1

Use the **Judy's magic cast-on** method (page 168) to cast on the number of stitches that you need for a toe-up sock or any other project that starts with a seamless cast-on edge.

Then work the "smoothing round".

STEP 2. SMOOTHING ROUND

2.1. Bring the **yarn to the back** of the work and **slip the first stitch** of the round purlwise from the left needle to the right needle.

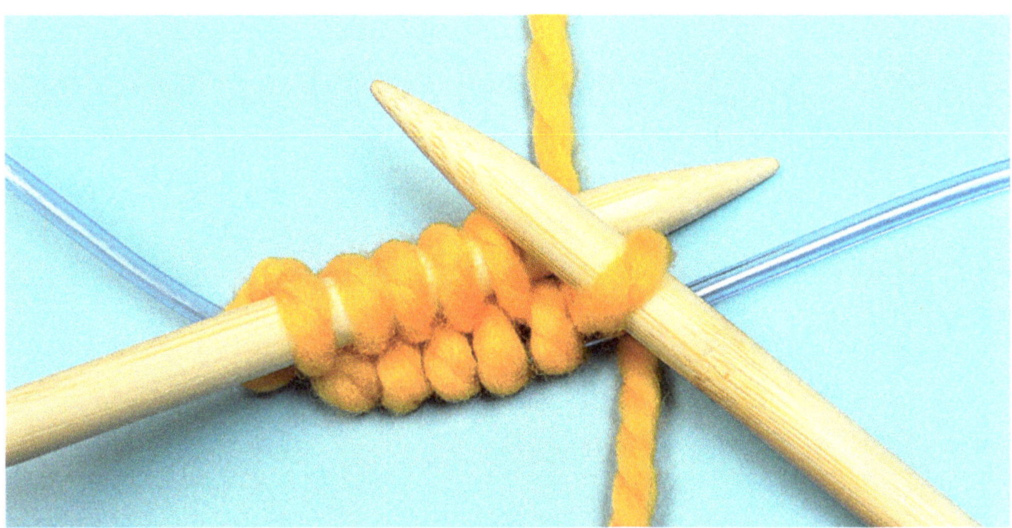

2.2. Work all stitches **to the last stitch of the first half** of the stitches.

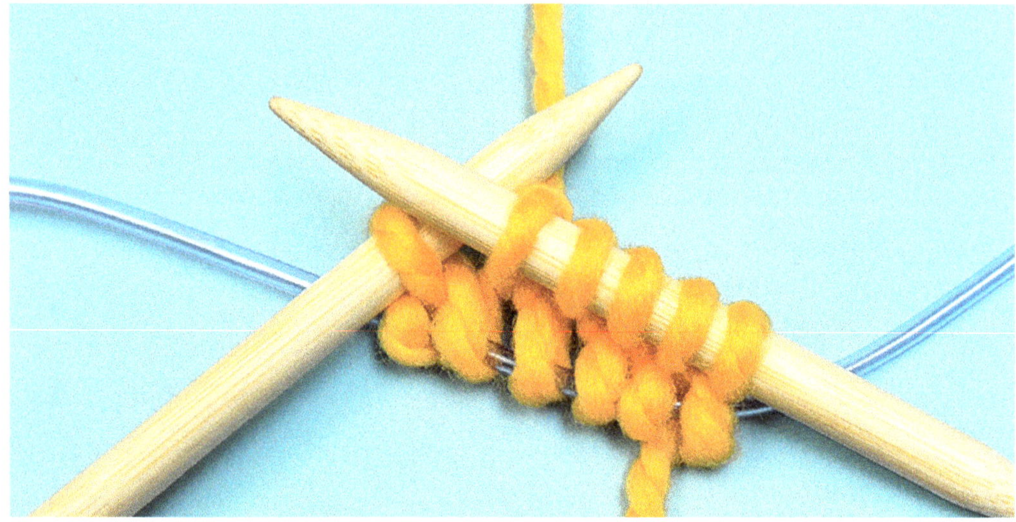

2.3. Slip the **last stitch of the first half** of the stitches. Do it purlwise with the yarn at the back of the work.

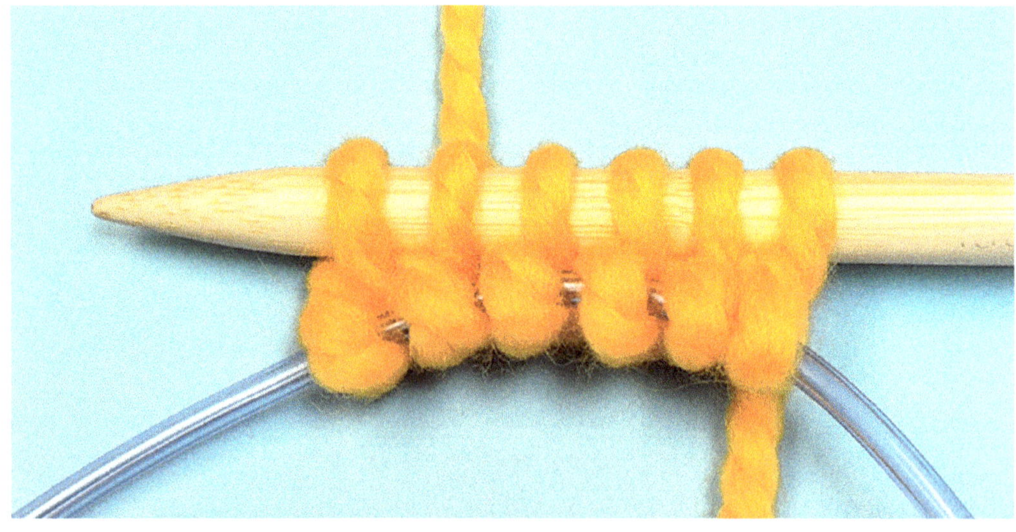

2.4. Repeat **steps 2 through 4** to work the **second half of the stitches** in a similar way—slipping the first and last stitches instead of knitting or purling them.

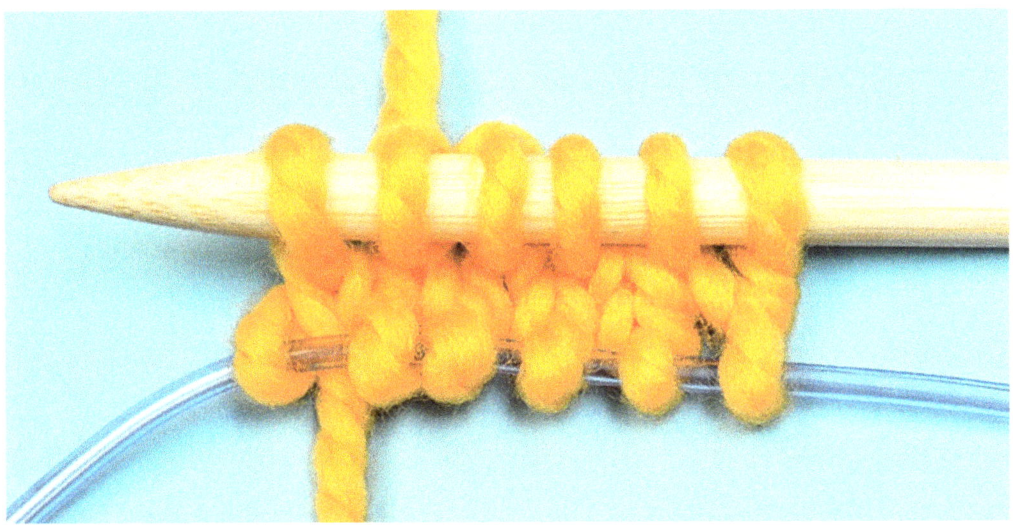

Starting with the next round, **follow the instructions of the pattern** that you use to make your project.

After you work a few rounds, you will see that there are no stitches sticking out at the sides of the cast-on edge. Instead, the **edge is nicely curved** and smooth.

I intentionally didn't add any shaping to my swatch. This way, you can see that this simple trick is powerful enough to even **soften the edges of a perfect rectangle**.

If you'd like to improve the look of the **edge finished by grafting** (page 176), work the **"smoothing round"** (step 2 described above) right before you bind off stitches.

Because we slip the edge stitches in the "smoothing round", we keep them **lower than the rest of the stitches** in that round. This simple trick tames those trouble-maker stitches and does not allow them to stick out at the sides of the edge.

TUBULAR CAST ON FOR 1X1 RIBBING

PART 1

Leave a tail at least 3 times as long as the cast-on edge. Place it on your left thumb and the working yarn on your left index finger.

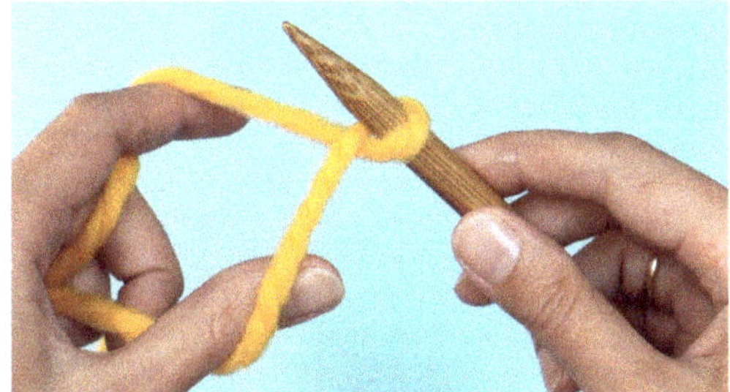

Move the needle down and to the right to create a loop by twisting the yarn. This loop is our first stitch.

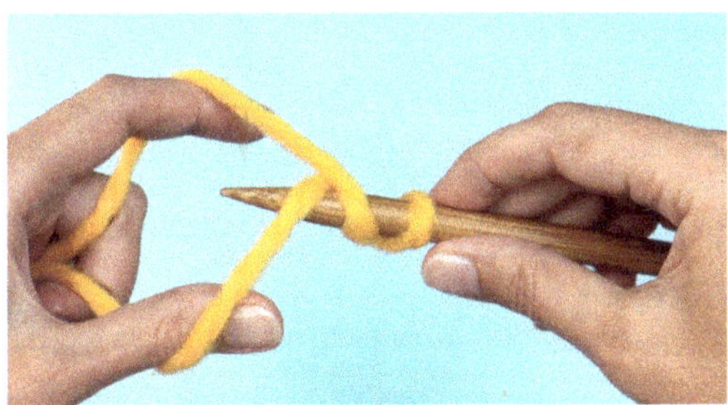

STEP 1. Pick the working yarn from right to left. Then pick the yarn tail from the bottom up.

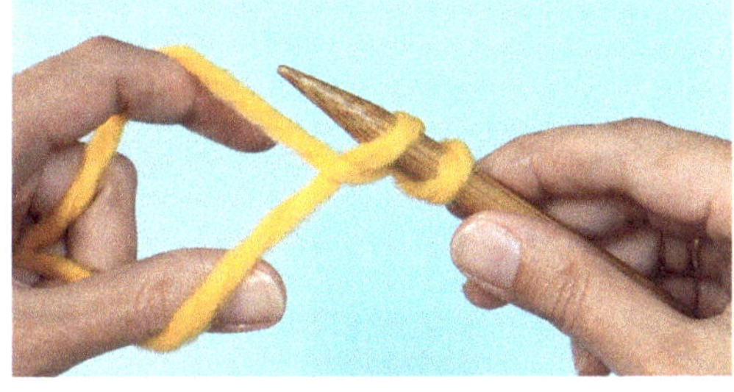

Move the needle from under the working yarn forming a new purl stitch. Make sure the stitch is tight.

STEP 2. Pick the yarn tail from the bottom up. Then pick the working yarn from right to left.

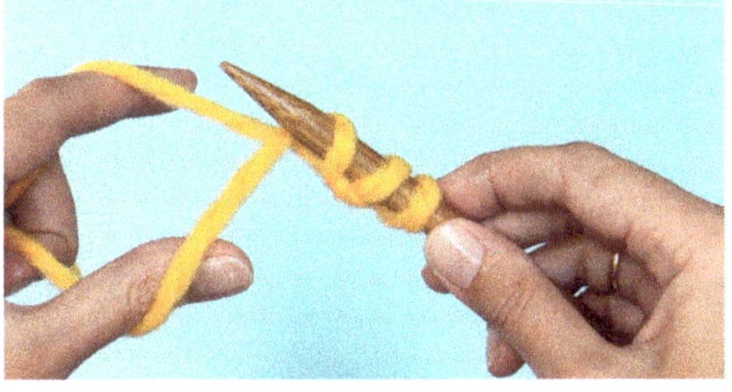

Move the tip of the needle from under the yarn tail, forming a new knit stitch. Keep the stitch tight.

TUBULAR CAST ON
FOR 1X1 RIBBING

PART 2

Repeat steps 1 and 2 to cast on all stitches. Twist the strands and turn the work.

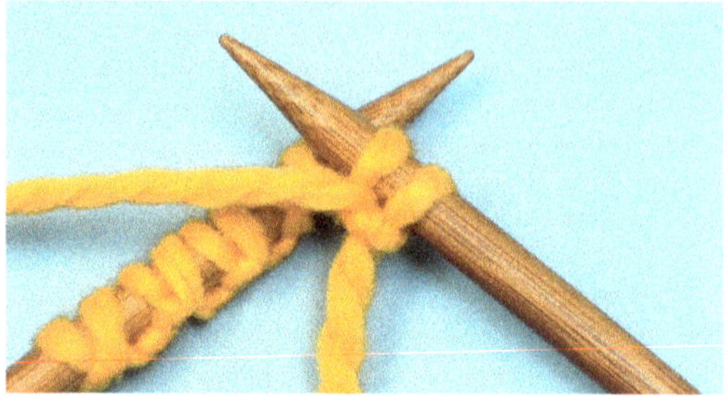

SETUP ROW 1. Knit the knit stitch through the back loop, slip the purl purlwise with yarn in front.

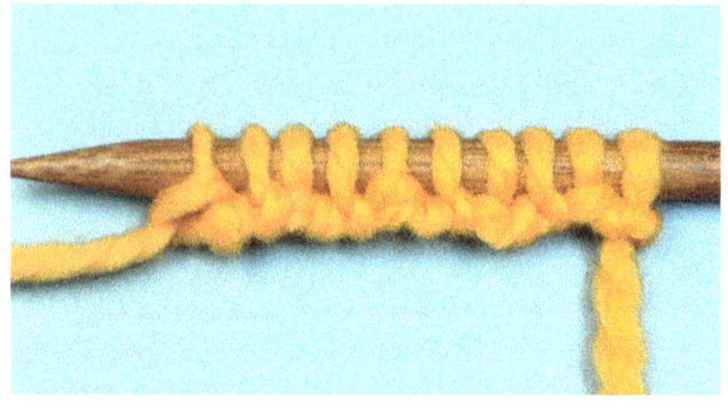

Repeat this sequence to the last two stitches. Knit 1 through the back loop and purl the last stitch.

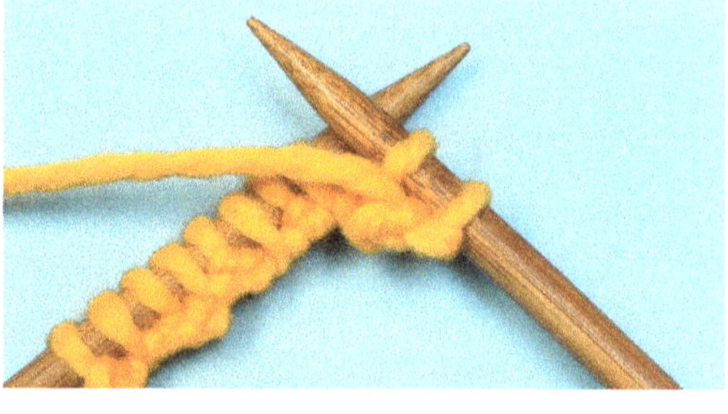

SETUP ROW 2. Knit the knit stitch through the front loop, slip the purl purlwise with yarn in front.

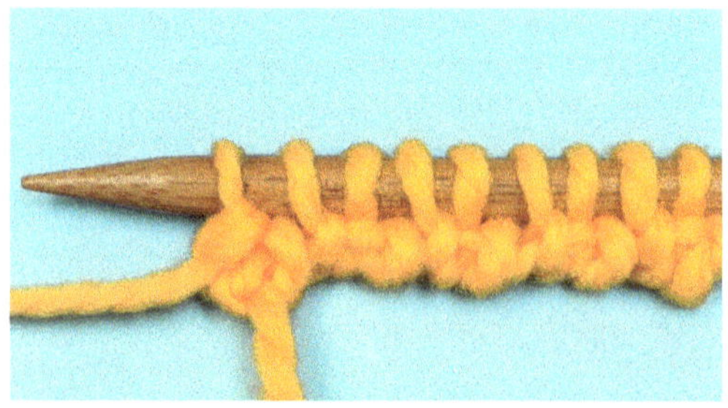

Repeat this sequence to the last two stitches. Knit 1 stitch and purl the last stitch.

The cast-on edge is now formed, and we can work in the classic 1x1 ribbing pattern.

TUBULAR BIND OFF
FOR 1X1 RIBBING

PART 1

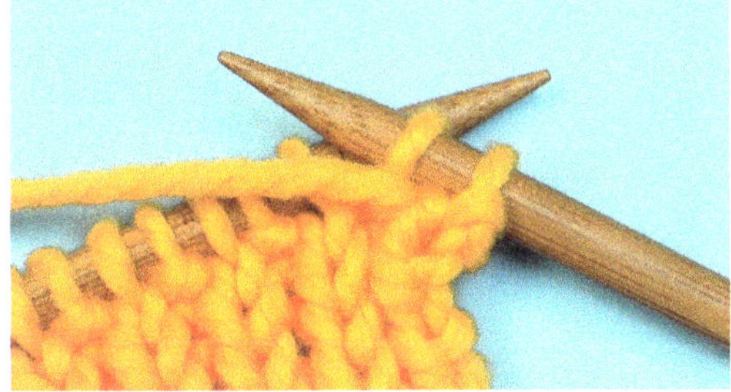

PREPARATION ROW 1. Knit the knit, slip 1 purlwise with yarn in front. Repeat to last stitch, purl 1.

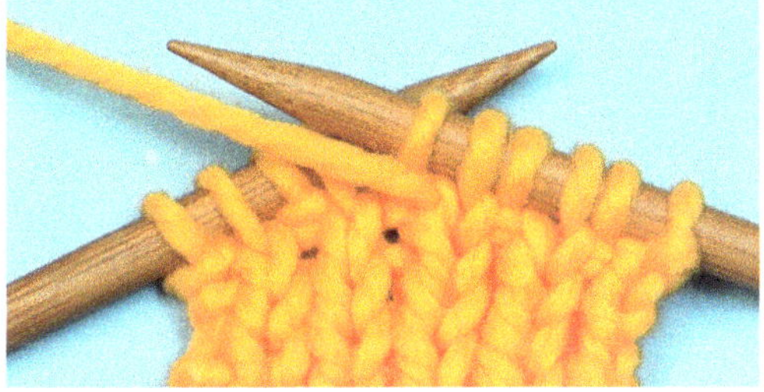

PREPARATION ROW 2. Work as the preparation row 1.

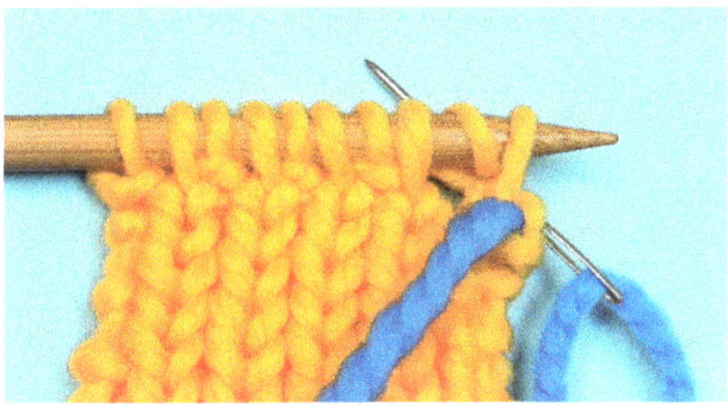

Leave a long tail and thread it into a wool needle. Insert the needle from left to right into the first purl stitch. Pull the yarn through.

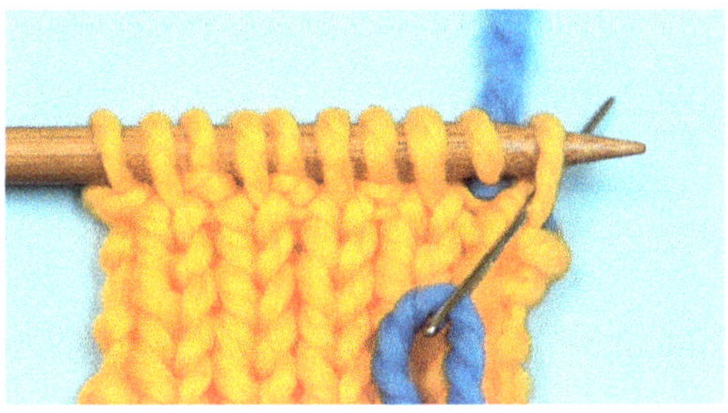

With the right side facing you, insert the wool needle from front to back into the first knit stitch.

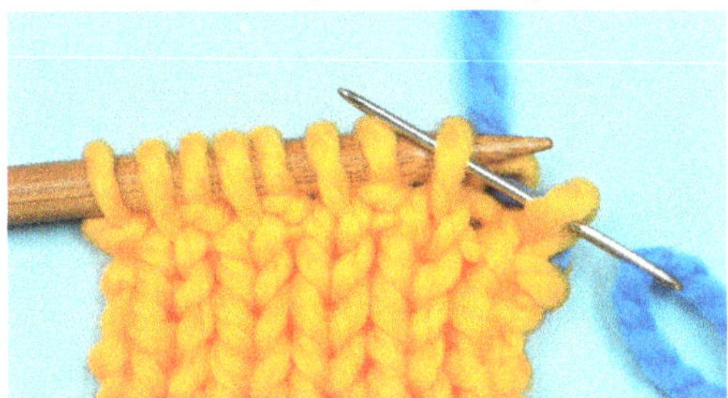

Drop this stitch and the "previously worked" purl stitch. Insert the needle from back to front into the next knit stitch.

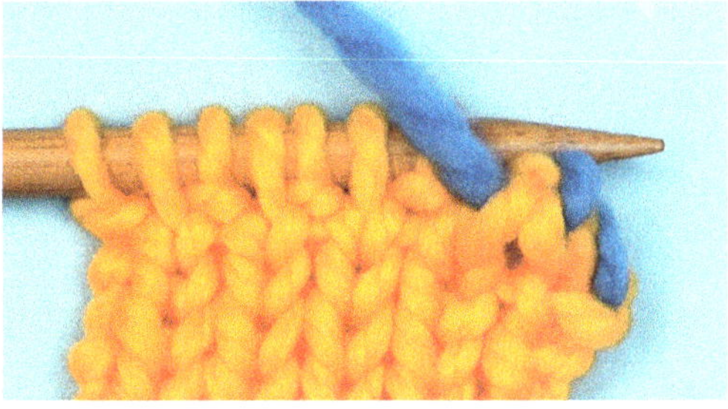

Drop this knit stitch and pull the yarn just enough to form a strand that is as long as one leg of an average stitch.

TUBULAR BIND OFF
FOR 1X1 RIBBING

PART 2

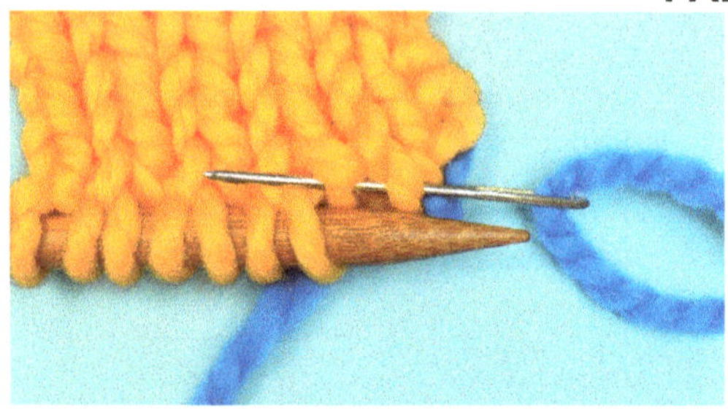

STEP 1. Rotate the fabric. Go front to back into the "previously worked" knit stitch, and back to front into the next knit stitch.

Slip this knit stitch off the knitting needle and pull the yarn through, forming a neat strand on top of the edge.

STEP 2. Rotate the fabric again. Go front to back into the "previously worked" knit stitch and back to front into the next knit stitch.

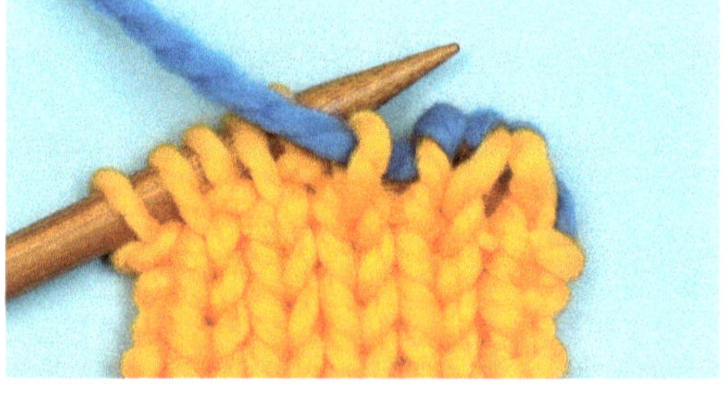

Slip the knit stitch off the knitting needle and pull the yarn through, forming a neat strand on top of the edge.

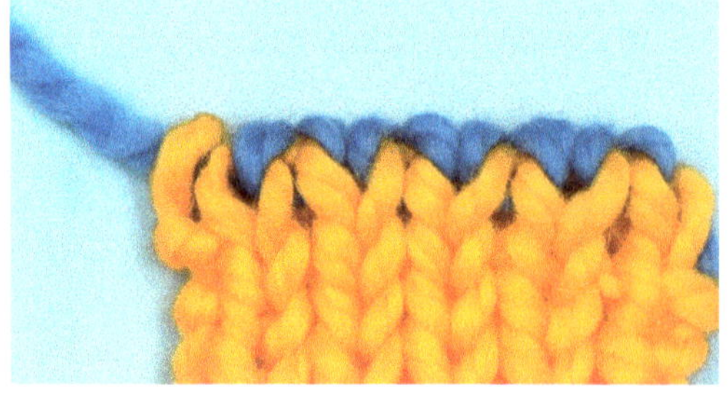

Repeat steps 1 and 2 until you bind off all stitches.

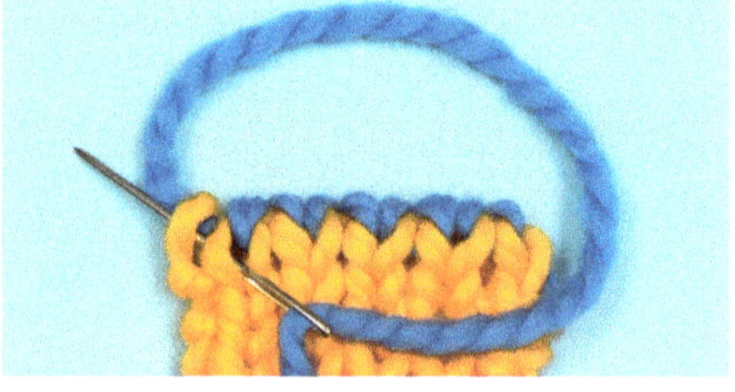

To finish, go from front to back into the last knit and the last purl stitches. Pull the yarn and secure.

TUBULAR CAST ON
FOR 2X2 RIBBING

PART 1

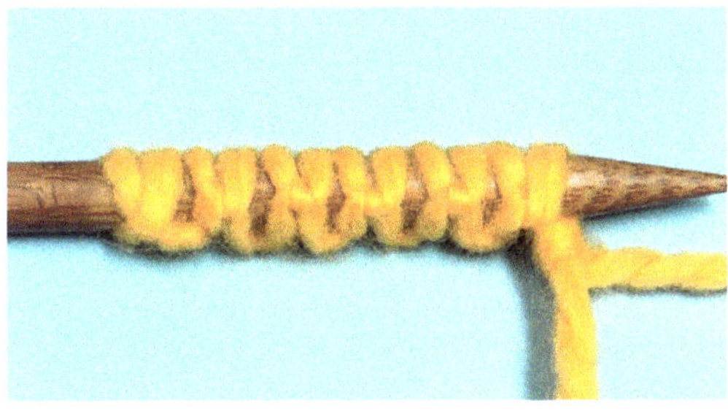

Use tubular cast on for 1x1 ribbing to cast on a multiple of 4 stitches.

SETUP ROW 1. [knit 1 through the back loop, slip 1 purlwise with yarn in front], repeat the brackets to the last stitch, purl 1.

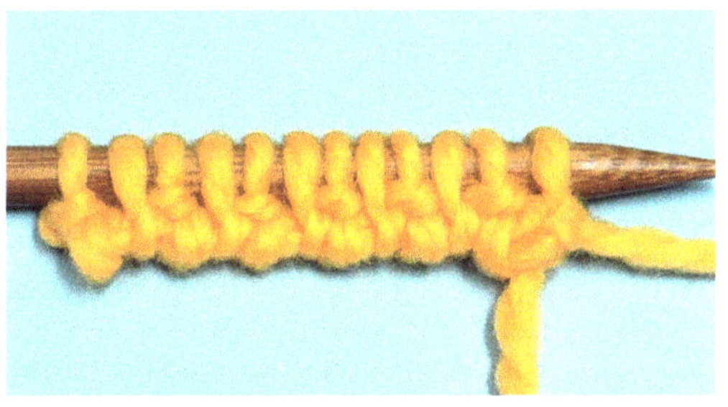

SETUP ROW 2. [knit 1, slip 1 purlwise with yarn in front], repeat the brackets to last stitch, purl 1.

SETUP ROW 3.

3.1. Knit 1 stitch.

3.2. Insert the right needle from left to right into the next two stitches as if to knit them together.

Ease the left needle out, slipping these stitches to the right needle.

TUBULAR CAST ON
FOR 2X2 RIBBING

PART 2

3.3. Return the slipped stitches back to the left needle. Do it purlwise, without twisting the stitches.

3.4. Knit 1 stitch through the back loop.

3.5. Purl 1 stitch through the back loop.

3.6 Purl the next stitch normally, through the front loop.

Repeat steps 3.1 through 3.6 to the end of the row.

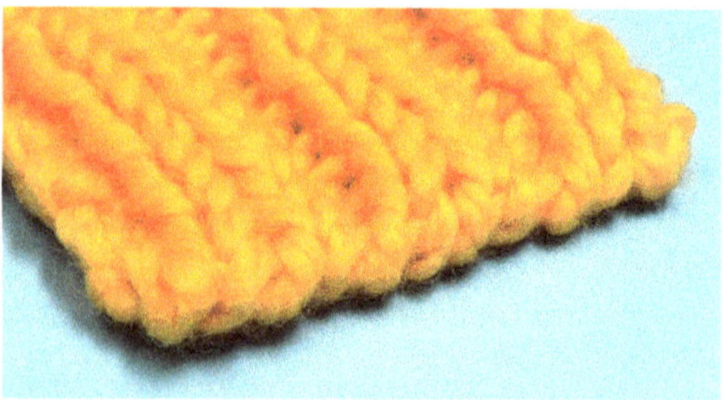

Work in the "knit 2, purl 2" ribbing pattern.

TUBULAR BIND OFF
FOR 2X2 RIBBING

PART 1

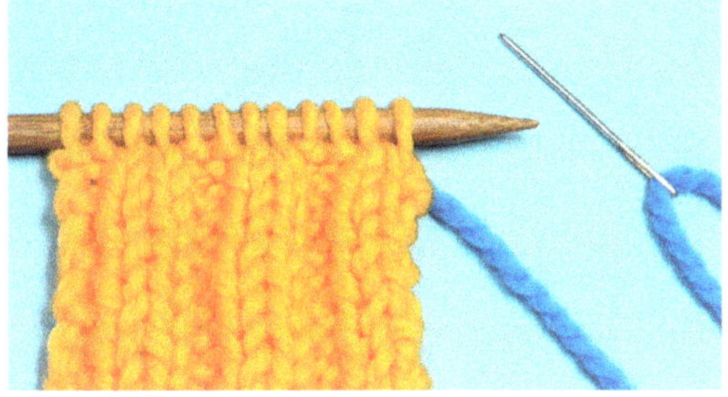

Leave a tail that is at least three times as long as the bind-off edge. Thread it into a wool needle.

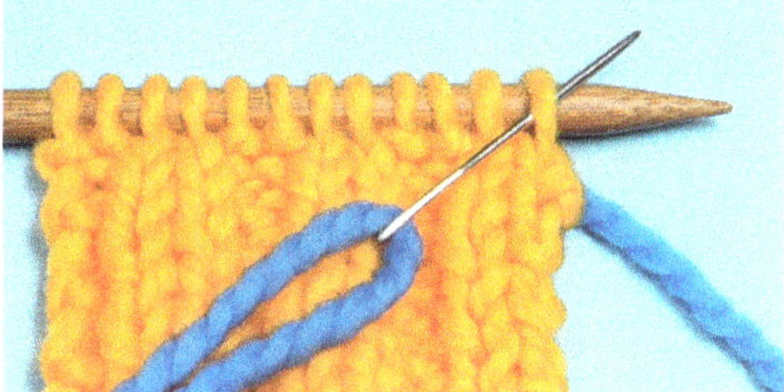

With the right side facing, insert the wool needle front to back into the first knit stitch.

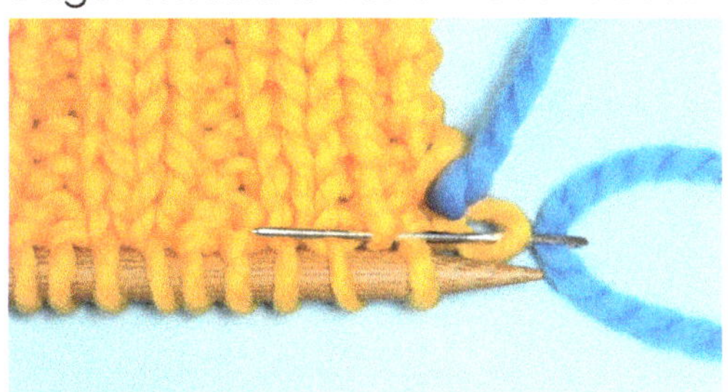

Drop this stitch. Rotate the fabric and go from back to front into the first knit stitch on the wrong side.

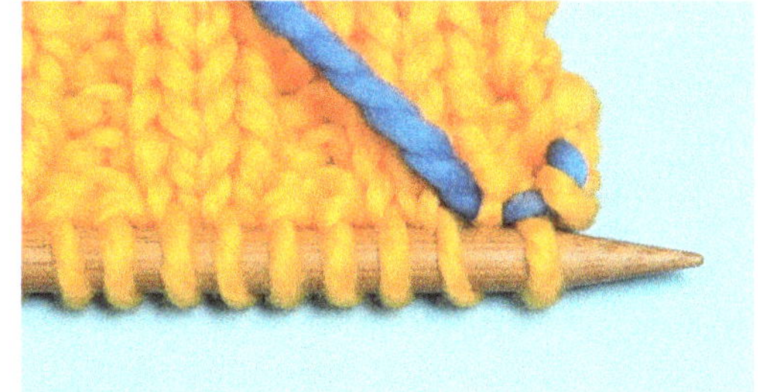

Pull the yarn through, forming a strand that is about as long as one leg of an average stitch.

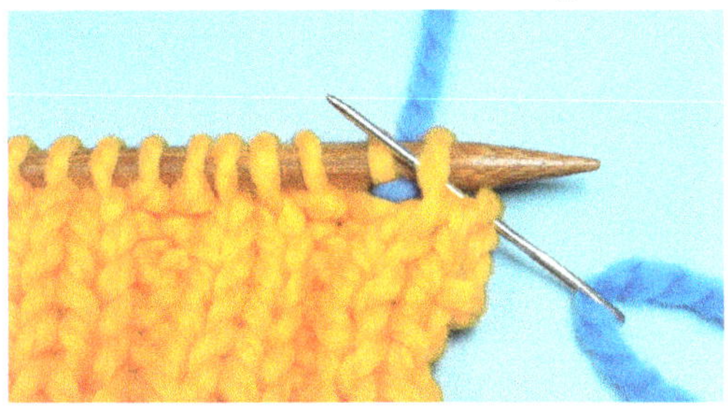

STEP 1. RIGHT SIDE. Go front to back into the "previously worked" knit stitch, and back to front into the next knit stitch. Drop this stitch. Pull the yarn through.

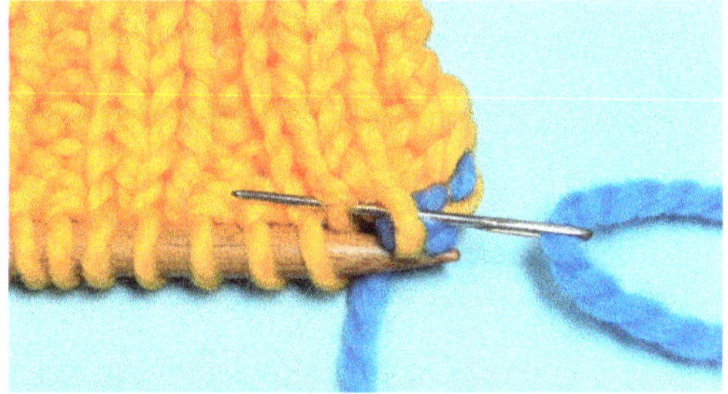

STEP 2. WRONG SIDE. Go front to back into the "previously worked" knit stitch. Drop this stitch and go back to front into the next knit stitch Drop this stitch. Pull yarn.

TUBULAR BIND OFF
FOR 2X2 RIBBING

PART 2

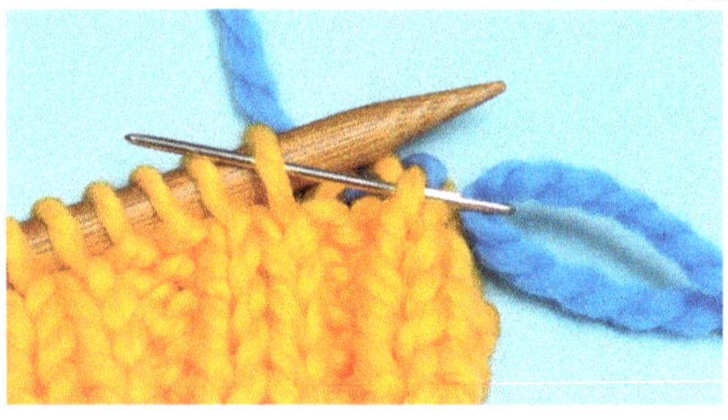

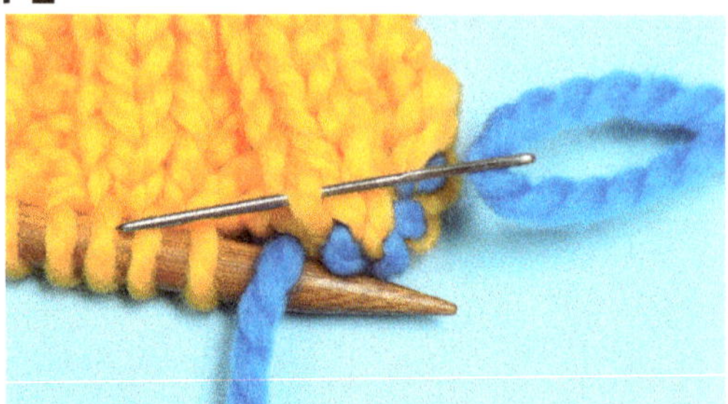

STEP 3. RIGHT SIDE. Go front to back into the "previously worked" knit and back to front into the next knit. Drop the stitch. Pull the yarn.

STEP 4. WRONG SIDE. Go front to back into the last knit stitch in the previous column of knit stitches.

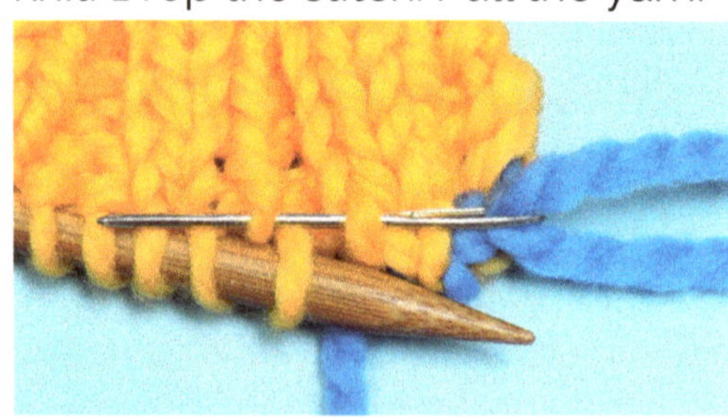

Go around the first stitch and insert the wool needle from back to front into the next knit stitch. Pull the yarn and form the strand.

Repeat steps 1 through 4 until you bind off all stitches.

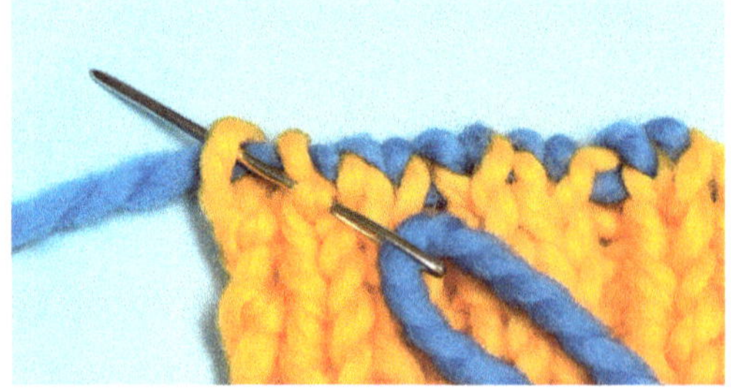

To finish, go front to back into the last knit on the right side and front to back into the last stitch of row.

Pull the yarn through and form the last strand on top of the edge.

JUDY'S MAGIC CAST ON

With two aligned needles in your right hand and the yarn tail in your left hand, place the yarn between the needles.

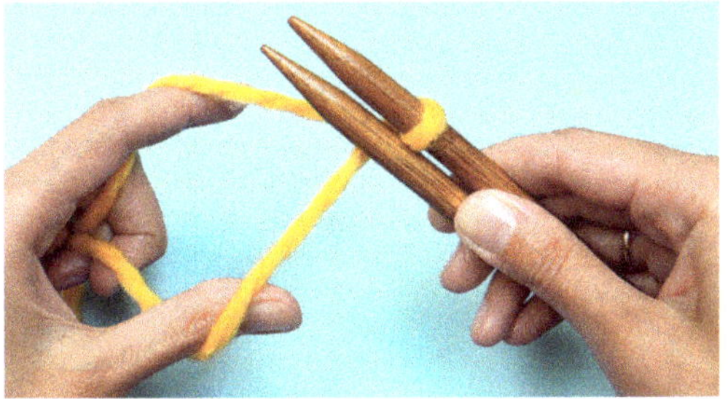

Move the yarn tail over the top needle. Place the tail on your left thumb and the working yarn on your left index finger.

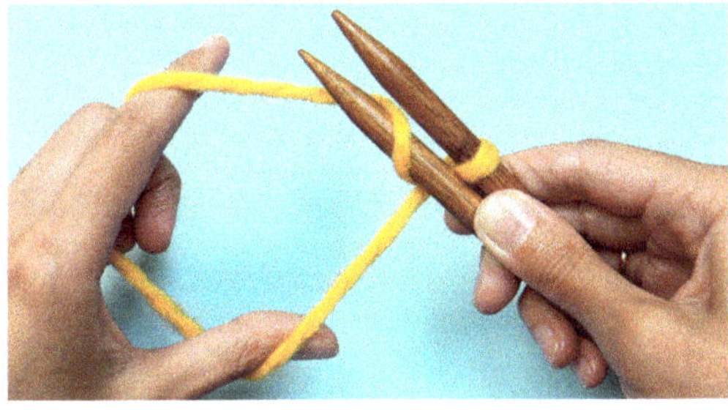

STEP 1. To add a stitch to the bottom needle, wrap the top strand around the bottom needle from front to back.

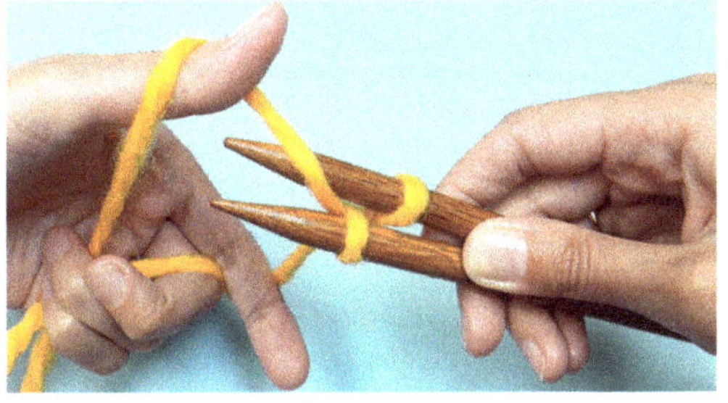

STEP 2. To add a stitch to the top needle, wrap the bottom strand around the top needle from front to back.

Repeat steps 1 and 2 until you cast on all stitches.

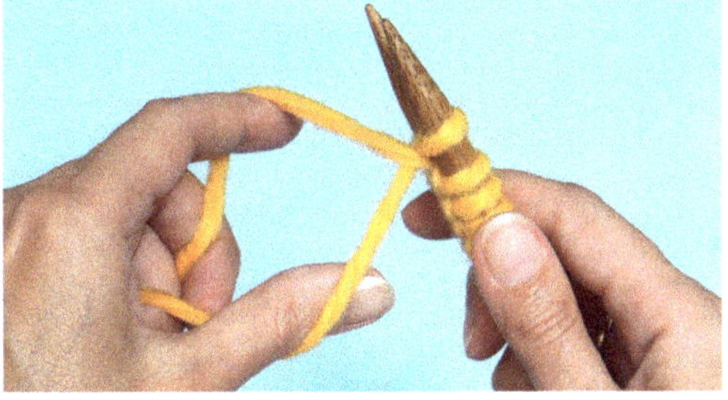

Twist the yarn tail and the working yarn to keep the last stitch from unravelling.

GRAFTING

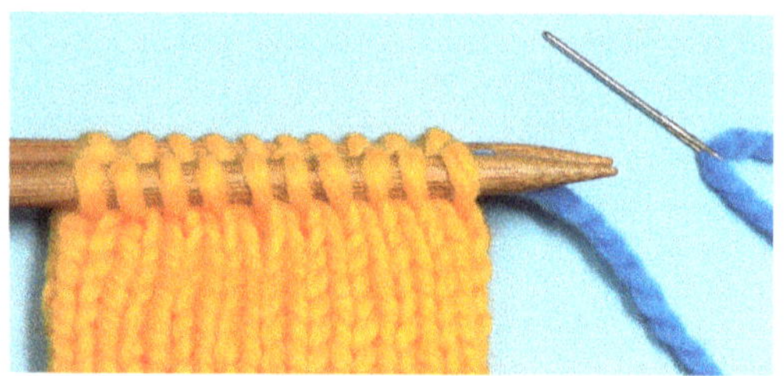

With one half of stitches on a needle at the front and the other half on a needle at the back, thread a long yarn tail into a wool needle.

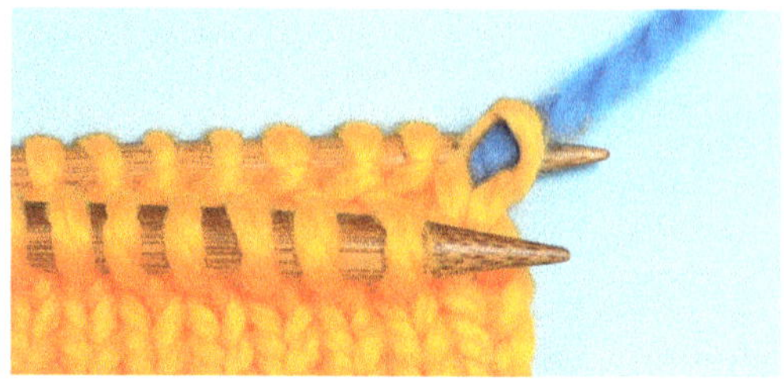

Go right to left into the 1st stitch on the front needle. Slip this stitch. Go left to right into the 1st stitch on the back needle. Slip this stitch, pull the yarn.

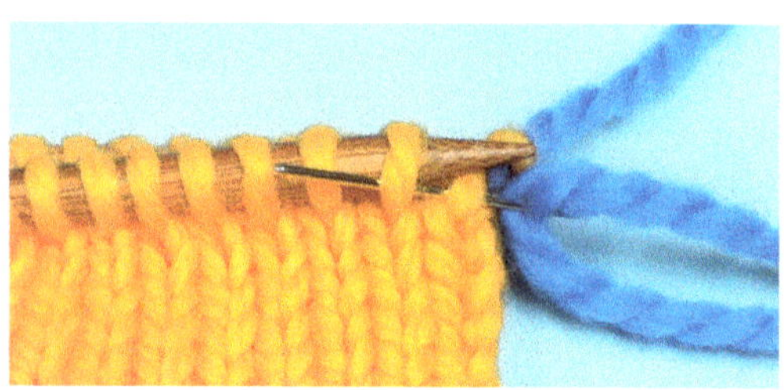

STEP 1. FRONT NEEDLE. Go front to back into the "previously worked" stitch and back to front into the next stitch.

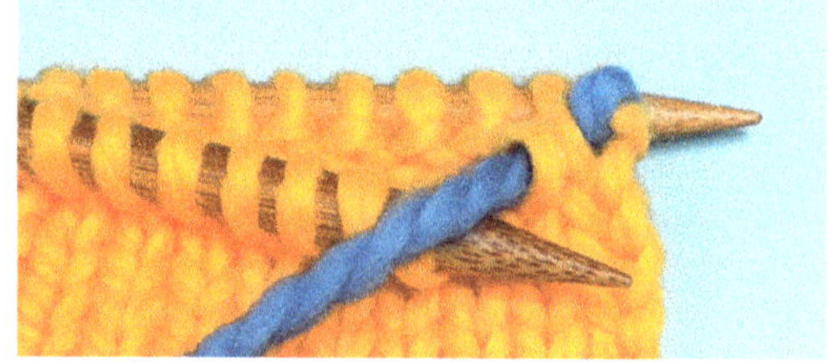

Slip this stitch off the knitting needle, pull the yarn through, and form a neat strand on top of the edge.

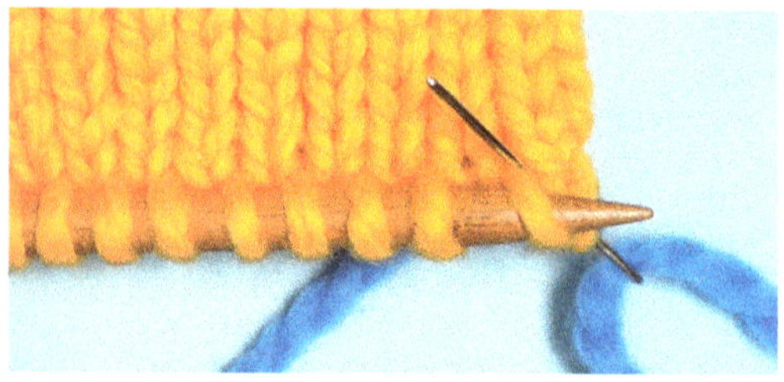

STEP 2. BACK NEEDLE. Rotate the fabric, then go front to back into the "previously worked" stitch and back to front into the next stitch.

Slip this stitch off the knitting needle and pull the yarn through, forming another strand on top of the edge.

Repeat steps 1 and 2 until you bind off all stitches.

BONUS

There is one more pair of matching cast-on and bind-off methods that I want to share with you., my friend.

I developed this duo during my quest for finding decorative ways to make horizontal edges.

These methods form highly-textured reversible scalloped edges that are perfect for blankets, shawls, and baby garments.

To download an e-book with the detailed step-by-step photo instructions that describe scalloped cast on and bind off methods,

go to **www.10rowsaday.com/scalloped-edges**

and use the password **BONUS.**

Happy knitting!

Maryna

There are more
knitting methods
to explore at
www.10rowsaday.com

Printed in the USA
CPSIA information can be obtained
at www.ICGtesting.com
LVHW070803081124
795954LV00015B/175